All Because of a Button
Folklore, Fact and Fiction

All Because of a Button

Folklore, Fact and Fiction

ELLARAINE LOCKIE

Heather Lockie, Illustrations

Foreword by Millicent Safro

ST. JOHANN PRESS
Haworth, NJ

ST. JOHANN PRESS

Published in the United States of America
P.O. Box 241
Haworth, NJ 07641

Copyright © 2000 by Ellaraine Lockie
All rights reserved.

Library of Congress Cataloging-in-Publication Data

Lockie, Ellaraine
    All because of a button : folklore, fact and fiction / Ellaraine Lockie ; Heather
Lockie, illustrations.
      p. cm.
    Includes bibliographical references and index.
    ISBN 1-878282-20-4 (alk. paper)
    1. Buttons—Collectors and collecting. 2. Buttons—Anecdotes. 3. Buttons—Folklore.
I. Title.

NK3668.5 .L63 2000
391.4'5'075—dc21

                                            00-062633

The paper used in this publication meets the minimum requirements of American National Standard for Information Sciences—Permanence of Paper for Printed Library Materials, ANSI/NISO Z39.48-1992

Manufactured in the United States of America

Dedication

This book is dedicated to all the button collectors since the 1930s who, through their persistent interest and thorough study of buttons and anything button related, have made the bulk of this book possible.

I thank the following:

The many button clubs and individuals throughout the world who so graciously shared their button experiences with me.

The National Button Society, British Button Society and California State Button Society for their cooperation.

Freddie Speights, editor of the *National Button Bulletin,* for running my "Button Bits" column, which collected book material.

The members of the Santa Clara Valley Button Club for their support.

The Sunnyvale and Mountain View Library Reference staffs for frequent research help.

Nancy Nehring, Margaret Kuechler, Karin Hesson, Bob Hesson, Lucille Weingarten and Bob Goligoski for proofreading the manuscript in its various stages.

Lawrence Green, SuAnn Kiser and Kevin Kiser for imparting research and writing skills.

Lucille Weingarten for her consistent inspiration, assistance, confidence and nonstop loans of rare buttons and books, magazines, newsletters and scrapbooks. The book would not have happened without her.

Dave Biesel, my smart and gentle publisher/editor, for adopting this book child, and Diane Biesel for her editing and support of the project.

My husband, Bob Goligoski, and my daughters, Heather and Shawn Lockie, for their constant support over the nine years during which I worked on the book. Special thanks to Heather for creating the illustrations. Buttons are hand drawn and artwork original except where copyrights are acknowledged.

Table of Contents

Dedication   v
Foreword—Millicent Safro   vii
Acknowledgments   ix
Introduction   1

All Because of a Button (A Button Made Them Do It)   3
Ambiguous Buttons (Buttons With Double Lives)   13
Versatile Buttons (Other Uses)   32
Buttons in the Bank (The Button Business)   56
Tall Tales About Tiny Buttons (Button Anecdotes)   66
Proper Buttons (Button Customs)   82
Charming Buttons (Charm Strings and Other Button Strings)   95
Button Buffs (Button Collectors)   102
Button Bigwigs (Buttons and Famous People)   112
Nuts and Bolts of Buttons (Materials, Subjects and Techniques)   121
Uniform Buttons That Went to War (And Ones That Stayed Home)   131
Button Gluttons (Buttons in Excess)   139
Buttons That Don't Button (Names, Places and Things)   146
Outlaw Buttons (Button Laws)   157
Literary Buttons (Buttons in Literature)   165
Button Talk (Button Expressions)   178
Funny Buttons (Button Jokes and Quotes)   183
Did You Know? (Fascinating Button Bits)   189

   Bibliography   199
   Index   201

Foreword

Small, round, intriguing, irresistible to some, utilitarian and overlooked by others, buttons have a long and fascinating history. As everyday fasteners, they reflect the materials, methods of manufacture, economic and aesthetic social structures of their day. They record historic and political events, fashion and decoration, styles of art and architecture, literature, theater and opera, popular stories and illustration. They include every possible material of the last two centuries, both natural and manufactured, from primitive stones to metal including gold, silver, pewter, brass, steel and tin, precious and semiprecious stones, mother-of-pearl, porcelain, pottery, ivory, bone, fabric, paper, leather, glass, and plastics.

As accessory and adornment as recorded in the 18th century, the so-called golden age of buttons, they defined wealth and bestowed social status. Buttons were produced mostly in Europe; in England, France, Austria, Germany, Hungary, Czechoslovakia, Italy, Holland, Ireland and Russia, and in America and as far away as Japan, Alaska and Africa.

Until now, there has been scant information about buttons as social artifacts. The earliest recorded use of the word "button" appeared in the 12th century "Chanson de Roland," in a disdainful phrase, comparing the button to pridefulness.

The earliest buttons were found in excavations in Egypt, Greece and Persia. Although their construction resembles modern buttons—with openings at the back—they were probably not used as fasteners, but as beads, badges, or ornaments.

Many portraits from the 16th and 17th centuries depict lavish displays of rows of ornamental buttons on gowns, sleeves, cuffs, inner and outer frock-coats and breeches of aristocratic men and women.

The height of art and politics of buttons flourished in the 18th century. Here more clearly than any other time, one can see the social and political structure of everyday life. The lavish and extravagant buttons worn by the nobility and, after the French Revolution, those worn by the emerging classes, became conspicuous, and increased in size and number. They were produced and embellished in a variety of materials, such as hand-painted porcelain, fabric elaborately embroidered in gold bullion and, most notably, carefully rendered miniature paintings under glass painted in the style of artists of the day.

In the 19th century, buttons contributed to the growing development of industrialization. As the new middle classes emerged, more buttons were produced, and women competed with men for decorative buttons and equal rights. Manufacture and machine production flourished in Europe and America and mass production made buttons inexpensive enough for all.

The 20th century brought new and brightly colored materials. Plastics were introduced by Leo Baekeland (Bakelite) and later, a new product, Catalin plastic, was produced in a greater variety of colors. Women adapted the four-hole button, previously used by men, for their blouses. The depression years of the 1930s yielded a spate of plastic, goofy and humorous buttons, seemingly to cheer things up.

Currently, in this environmentally friendly modern millennium, corozo nut, so-called vegetable ivory buttons, a popular material used in early 20th century button production, is once again in demand. Here again, the button made from a natural material is being used as a cultural and social artifact affecting the economics of the day. Hence, the button will help save the planet.

It is with a touch of humor that we approach collecting of obscure and insignificant objects. It is not surprising then that these relics of the past are desired by collectors from around the world. What is surprising and also amusing is the vast number of people who are attracted to the notion of learning history from a button.

In this book, Ms. Lockie examines the historical and current impact that buttons have made on society. Convincingly, she suggests to the reader that buttons are not so insignificant after all! She goes beyond the historical aspect of buttons and delves into their sociological and psychological consequences. This book reflects a most interesting slant on the subject and is the most extensive study of button-related social phenomena to date.

—Millicent Safro

Acknowledgments

Information for this book came from hundreds of sources: interviews, books, magazines, periodicals, newspapers, movies, television, museums, organizations, letters, newsletters and scrapbooks. Frequently used sources were numerous United States button club publications, *The National Button Bulletin*, California State Button Society's scrapbooks, British Button Society's archives, *Button Lines*, *Just Buttons*, *Hobbies* and *Western Button News*.

The following is a list of individuals who contributed material:

Ita Aber, Margaret Acker, Constance Alexander, Roxanne Ashley, Lorrayne Bailey, Alice M. Banta, Caryl Beck, Gil Biggie, Shelia M. Bird, David Bittner, Martha Blackwell, Anne Blight, Todd Brix, Sidney P. Bloomberg, Dorine Braun, Florence M. Brill, Juanita Case, Shirley Case, Angela Clark, Betty Cross, Margie Crow, Jennifer Curtis, Carol A. Darling, Gladys Davis, George Dawson, Thomas Duran, Helene Elko, Mary D. Fafinski, Diane Ford, Sandra Foster, Henry H. Franklin, Martyn Frith, Claire Garrity, Pat Garvey, Ty Geltmaker, Cathe Giffuri, Bryan Gilbert, Larry Golding, Fern Goodal, Robert and Marjorie Goodwin, Wilda Gould, Marilyn Green, Roma Greth, Edith S. Guetz, Dr. and Mrs. A. T. Hall, Omid Hashemi, George E. Hatvary, Fay Hayward, Joan M. Helton, Lorna Herrington, June and Walter Hirsch, Robert F. Hobbs, Tomi Horne, Peter Hyypio, Marc Jacobs, Diane Jahnke, Catherine Jensen, Sara Joelson, Thelma Johns, Allen Johnson, Glenys Johnson, Irene Johnson, Jehovina M. Kelsall, William Kennedy, Polly Kirlin, Eugene R. Klompus, Dorothy E. Knox, John E. Knox, Linda Kupecek, Gertrude Langsam, June Lawrence, Louise Leisch, Rachel Leslie, Andrea Llewellyn, Marion Magee, Janel Marchi, Thomas Markos, H. B. Martin, Ruth H. Martin, Stella McCowen, Sonja Medcalf, Pauline Moody, Marie J. Moore, Nancy Nehring, Norman Odlum, Helyn Reeves Olds, Jeanne Ordelman, Peggy Ann Osborne, Christa Petraskova, Johanna Rauhala, Dorothy Ryder, Millicent Safro, Cynthia Sanchez, Shirley Schilling, Oscar Shefler, Sarah M. Sieger, M. W. "Freddie" Speights, Marge Spieldenner, Grace Spohn, Mary Ann Spychalski, Aude Staalman-Boer, Ellen Stafford, Louise Start, Bonnie Thompson, Warren Tice, Lodoscia Trost, Doroty Tunison, Gerald J. Walker, Yvonne Ward, Beau Warrick, Kathie Webb, Lucille Weingarten, Arlene Westrom, Janet White, Roger White, Sherry White, William M. White, Alice Willson, Faye Wolfe, Valera Wright, Annabell Yurutucu, Barbara Yarberry, Jean Young.

All Because of a Button

Folklore, Fact and Fiction

Introduction

When I was a little girl I played with baby food jars full of buttons in my mother's sewing closet. Growing up, I saved every button I could find. As a young adult, I covered clothes with buttons, made jewelry with them and filled my own jars with them. I just couldn't get enough of those brightly colored, plastic winsome little devices.

That is, until one day when I walked into Jerry Fine's Antiquewear store in Marblehead, Massachusetts. Covering the walls and table tops were thousands of antique buttons, each with its own written history. There was not one modern plastic button among them.

After a cursory look around, the prices shocked me into leaving. I had never before paid more than twenty-five cents for a used button and had never heard of "antique buttons."

I didn't leave fast enough, though, because over lunch I kept thinking about a fabulous large brass and steel button that had been made into a brooch. It depicted a breathtakingly beautiful, romantic scene with Pierrot and Pierrette and was called "True Love." The history said it represented a scene from the French pantomime theater in 1896. By the time I finished eating, I told my husband we had found my Christmas present!

I took him back to Antiquewear with a mental vow to grab "True Love," pay for it and make another quick exit so as to avoid buying my next ten Christmas presents.

Of course this didn't work. There were exquisite hand-painted buttons by famous bygone artists, buttons with semiprecious jewels, gold, metals of silver and copper that were engraved, lithographed and enameled, steel that was faceted to resemble marcasite, shell, pearl, ivory and horn that were inlaid and carved, tintype buttons from the Civil War, military buttons from all the nineteenth century wars, glass that was cut, pressed and blown and ceramic buttons of porcelain and china.

Subjects included famous and infamous people and important events throughout history, stories, fairy tales, illustrations from books and magazines of the day, historical buildings, sporting scenes, theater, opera, mythology, animals, birds, zodiacs, flowers, plant life and much more.

The store was a museum of miniature art that exuded history. These buttons read like journals of our ancestors' lives and of events going back hundreds of years. Every craft, art, science, custom, subject and industry was reflected in them.

At the end of the day, I was mesmerized, infatuated, and totally in love with antique buttons. I began to think they were the best antique buys in America . . . inexpensive really, and they came with their own researched histories!

I left enriched with far more than my "True Love" brooch, which remains to this day my signature piece of jewelry.

As captivated as I was with the intrinsic beauty of material, workmanship, design and rich history of antique buttons, I gradually became aware of yet another dimension surrounding these historical and artistic treasures—their impact on people throughout history and in the present. Buttons are full of legends, stories, facts and fancies.

Their impact on social interactions between individuals and between cultures and the way they have slipped into so many aspects of our lives intrigued me. I began to collect stories and interesting tidbits about buttons. Some were funny, amusing and almost unbelievable. Others were shocking, sad and thought-provoking.

The result of my collection of button-related phenomena is this book, which after reading, will not allow you to think of buttons as merely things that come off in the wash. Rather, I hope you'll think of them as tiny, masterful periscopes to the past and fascinating reflections of all facets of life in the present.

People ask me, "But what *is* button folklore?" sometimes with a look that suggests I've "lost my buttons." I give them this analogy: Button folklore is like a bunch of beautiful women. You could write a book on how exquisite they look, where they came from and how they were put together. That's the format for most button books. But you also could write a book on where they've been, what uses they've served and what impacts they've had on the world. And that's the format for this book.

All Because of a Button
(A Button Made Them Do It)

Buttons have caused all kinds of surprising events. They have been directly responsible for saving lives and causing deaths. They have brought wealth to their owners as well as hospital bills. They have caused divorces, phobias and job resignations. They have testified in courts, solved crimes and started industries and riots.

We all know that buttons are the little heroes that hold our clothes together, but they have also been the culprits that have exposed some of us in the most unlikely ways.

The incidents related here illustrate a sample of the profound effects buttons have had on our lives.

Some of the people whose lives have been saved by buttons throughout history have been famous. When George Frederick Handel was a young man, he played the harpsichord in the opera "Cleopatra" at the Hamburg Opera House. Johann Mattheson, a friend of Handel's, had composed the opera and conducted it. He also sang the principal role, but his character died before the last act of the opera. It was Mattheson's custom to replace Handel at the harpsichord for the last act. One evening Handel refused to give up his place. The two men quarreled, and the result was a sword duel outside the theater. During the duel, Mattheson made a lunge at Handel's heart, but his sword broke without harming Handel because it splintered on a large metal button on Handel's coat. Handel lived to write the beloved "Messiah."

A button saved the life of Andrew Jackson, the seventh president of the United States, when Jackson and a man named Charles Dickinson fought a duel of honor in Kentucky. Both were expert marksmen, but Dickinson was considered slightly better. The night before the duel, Jackson's best friend, a Mr. Overton, advised him to wear a coat on which large silver buttons formed a decorative pattern. The morning of the duel, Mr. Dickinson took aim and fired at Jackson's heart. Jackson fired back. Dickinson was mortally wounded. Jackson survived with a severely bruised chest and several broken ribs. His life had been spared by a silver button which, on the night before, Overton had removed and resewn on Jackson's coat directly over the heart.

Another button is said to have saved the life of a handsome and charming Frenchman named Georges d'Anthès in the days of Czar Nicholas' court in Russia. D'Anthès became romantically involved with the wife of Alexander Pushkin, the great poet, and this resulted in a duel between the two men. D'Anthès was a crack shot and hit Pushkin in his abdomen. Pushkin propped himself up and fired a shot that hit d'Anthès in the chest. But a button deflected the bullet, so d'Anethès suffered only two broken ribs and an arm wound. Pushkin died two days later.

A few buttons might have averted World War I if Archduke Francis Ferdinand of Austria, whose assassination in Sarajevo started the war, had been wearing them. The Archduke had a practice of always having himself sewed into his uniform. When he was shot, he bled to death because aides could not remove his coat fast enough to tend his wounds. Total casualties from the war were nearly ten million, and the wounded totaled twenty-one million.

Buttons have been responsible for unfortunate and even tragic events. When silk button makers rioted in Macclesfield, England, in 1737, the riots were directly due to the introduction of woven buttons. There was a law in effect forbidding the making and wearing of covered buttons, and woven buttons were to be exempt from this law, which caused violent behavior from other fabric button makers.

Paul, son of Peter III and Catherine II of Russia, was reviewing his troops in 1799 when he saw a button missing from a soldier's uniform. Enraged, he ordered an about-face and sent 400 men off on a 2,000-mile march to Siberia. They had no food or supplies and were never heard from again.

Pants fell from a group of Napoleon's soldiers during the winter retreat from Russia in 1812 because their tin buttons changed crystal structure in the freezing temperature and disintegrated into a fine powder, leaving the soldiers with nothing to hold up their pants.

Another uniform trouser loss occurred during World War II when braces buttons (suspender buttons to Americans) were issued to the British troops. The buttons were poorly made and had sharp edges that cut the threads used to stitch them onto uniforms. Consequently, the braces became detached from the trousers, and the trousers fell.

Civilians, too, have had trouble keeping on their clothes due to button betrayal. A woman was once standing with a group on a railroad station platform near Chicago on a very cold winter day. When the train pulled in, steam covered the woman; and to everyone's dismay, the buttons on the front of her coat just disappeared with the steam. They simply vanished, leaving only the threads on the woman's clothes. The buttons had been made of dried ox blood and were blue. Bystanders contributed safety pins to the unfortunate woman. (The buttons were probably made of tin. See the button with plaque explanation on page 71.)

A more serious consequence occurred when a man purchased a set of pure gold ones with the Iranian crest on them at the Tender Buttons store in New York City during the deposing of the Shah of Iran. When the man wore the buttons in Washington D. C., he was attacked and beaten by a group of protesters. Bruised, he returned the buttons to Tender Buttons and asked for a refund, which he was given.

Buttons have been the cause of medical emergencies. In 1941, Helen Terry from Colorado missed an unusual button that she had cherished since childhood. Joyce, her three-year-old daughter, knew where the button was, but she kept it a secret until it began to hurt. The heirloom button was lodged in her nose. At the Denver hospital three surgeons removed the button from the little girl's nose.

More recently Roxanne Ashley, a button collector in California reported that she didn't take her four-year old son to the doctor on such an occasion. She performed the "button-ectomy" with a tweezers herself and removed an old shoe button from his nose.

Inanimate objects have also had button trouble. In 1783, the French Montgolfier brothers, inventors of the hot air balloon, made a large balloon for a public demonstration that took place at Annonay. The balloon rose to 6,000 feet and was forced to land ten minutes later, a mile and a half away. Different parts of the balloon were fastened together with buttons, and the short duration of the flight was the result of gas lost through the buttonholes.

In 1790 in France, buttons were responsible for the defacing of books. In that year a book was published to commemorate the taking of the Bastille. The book contained pictures of a set of eighteen small, colored engravings designed by Guyot. The little pieces of art were mounted and sold as buttons. One newspaper stated that three thousand pages containing these illustrations had been torn out of the books to be used for buttons.

Buttons have been the reason some people have committed crimes. In nineteenth century England, a kindly sheepherder named John Lloyd was known as "Silver John the Bonesetter." He mended broken bones of people in his community. As thanks for his administering, the people gave him silver buttons which he wore on his coat. Eventually his coat was covered with them, and he reserved the wearing of this coat for special occasions and whenever he attended to broken bones. After one of these occasions, Silver John didn't return to his farm. That winter his body, minus the coat, was found under a sheet of ice on a lake. His body was removed the following spring. It became evident that he was murdered and thrown into the lake for his silver buttons.

The Times in London reported in 1976 that Nottinghamshire police were searching for a burglar who shot a pet dog and killed it. The dog had tackled the burglar who broke into a house and stole a collection of gold buttons.

More recently, Felicidad Noriega, wife of deposed Panamanian dictator Manuel Noriega, was arrested for shoplifting buttons at a Miami boutique. According to the police report, Mrs. Noriega was watched as she and another woman cut buttons off ten jackets in the shop. The value of the twenty-seven buttons taken was said to be $305.00. The damage was estimated to be $1,242.87.

Another publicized button theft was committed by Mariolina Fassino in England. Ms. Fassino, who sold second-hand clothes at a stall in Brick Lane Market in London, bought a used Versace jacket for one and one-half pounds sterling, but it was missing a few buttons. Miss Fassino received a 1,650 pounds sterling fine for vandalizing designer jackets to replace the missing buttons. She had taken a pair of scissors into the Cecil Gee store on Oxford Street and snipped eleven buttons from Versace clothes before she was apprehended.

According to *The Telegraph,* Miss Fassino said, "It seems a high price for what I did. How do they expect me to pay for all that? With buttons?"

Buttons have negatively impacted people's mental health and sense of well being. In 1988, bride-to-be Linda Newell nearly called off her engagement when she discovered her fiancee wore pajamas with buttons, according to the *Sunday Mirror* in England. She suffered from koumphiphobia, a terror of buttons, and couldn't bear the thought of coming face to face with a row of buttons in the night.

Miss Newell, whose clothes fastened with velcro, said that the phobia started when she was a child. Suddenly she began to feel nauseous when she was buttoning up her coat or blouse. "Now I have to look away when I see a man wearing a shirt without a tie," she said.

Ellen Staffor in Ontario, Canada, has suffered from button phobia ever since she can remember. As a child, she couldn't bring herself to wear a gift of a pretty dress that had buttons down the front of it. As an adult, she dressed her children in buttonless clothes and has always managed to keep herself clothed without resorting to buttons. To her they are "the equivalent of cockroaches . . . something to be avoided at all costs."

Aude Stallman-Boer from Holland once asked a merchant at a collector's fair if he sold buttons in his stall. He replied with horror that he had been afraid of buttons since childhood. He didn't fear buttons that were sewn onto something, only loose buttons.

Martyn Frith, owner of The Button Queen store in London, has also had experience with button phobias. He has known a half dozen people with the problem. Once he was introduced by a chaplain to a woman as "The Button Queen" at a wedding in Glasgow. The woman leaped away, refusing to shake hands with him because she was terrified of buttons. People have come into his store, when their companions have stood across the street because of their fear of buttons.

Some people are merely superstitious about buttons. Duke Ellington once delayed a concert for thirty-five minutes while his assistants looked for a shirt with no buttons for him.

Communal and marital relationships have also suffered because of buttons. *Reader's Digest* reported that a judge was none too lenient with George Twiller in divorce court because he put his wife over his knees and spanked her with a folded magazine for her button behavior. George Twiller said his wife collected buttons . . . pearl buttons, glass buttons, wooden buttons, leather buttons. She had political buttons dating back to William Henry Harrison. Twiller didn't object when she snipped the bronze buttons from his grandfather's Civil War uniform, nor when she pried the buttons off the living room sofa; but when she cut off the copper rivets from his fishing dungarees, he struck her.

Conflicts over buttons have erupted in diverse age brackets and in varied locales. Once in rural America, a fight over buttoning led to an outhouse disaster. When Louise Start was three years old and her brother was five, they had a "two seater" outdoor toilet. One day they were both using it when she finished first, stood in front of him and asked him if he would button her sunsuit straps.

He refused. She was so upset she gave him a push and down the hole he went! Louise ran to her mother and told her what happened. Her mother grabbed a broom, ran to the outhouse and frantically pulled him out.

A dispute over how many buttons a girl should wear on her blazer lead to the resignation of two school governors and an offer to resign from the head of the school in England, reported *The Times* in 1990. Disagreement started when the eleven-year old girl came to school with three buttons on her blazer instead of the regulation two, and her parents were told she would be banned from school. When they protested, the governors backed the parents, and the school's chief official offered to resign. Two governors later resigned because of the way the whole affair was handled. The girl was allowed to wear her three-button blazer until it wore out, and then it would be replaced by a blazer with the correct number of buttons.

Buttons have compensated for their negative impacts on society, however. There are several known instances where buttons have identified criminals. Such an incident involved Tom Quick, a legendary character in New York State, who got help from buttons to identify his father's killer. Quick went into a tavern in Neversink one night a couple of years after the French and Indian Wars. An Indian named Muskwink was drinking and boasting of his exploits in the war. Muskwink showed off a set of fine silver buttons taken from a victim. Quick recognized the buttons as having belonged to his father. Muskwink told of killing the buttons' owner. Quick grabbed a musket from the wall and forced Muskwink up the road where Quick shot him to death and pocketed the silver buttons.

Another instance was in the 1880s in New Orleans when a respected butcher named Hans Mueller allegedly murdered his wife by pushing her into a huge meat grinder. Mrs. Mueller had grown old and wrinkled before her time, and it was said that the butcher fell in love with a young administrative assistant. When customers complained about broken buttons and bits of fabric in sausages from Mueller's meat market a few days after Mrs. Mueller's disappearance, the police were alerted. When a piece of gold wedding ring was found in a sausage, Mueller was arrested. He never stood trial, however, because he began seeing his wife's ghost and was committed to an insane asylum where he eventually committed suicide.

In 1965, a button was held as evidence in the trial of George Whitmore. He was accused of attacking a woman named Elba Borrero, who said she tore the button from his coat during the attack. A button was missing from Whitmore's coat when he was arrested, and the remaining ones matched the button Ms. Borrero had.

Buttons were the proof leading the fire department to suspect arson and murder when the Taylor & Johns Company store burned down with the senior partner Sam Taylor inside. The junior partner Willard Johns claimed Taylor was working late and had fallen asleep with a lit cigarette in his hand.

The store stock had consisted of thousands of dollars worth of men's suits. The fire department might have believed John's theory except that no buttons were found among the ashes. If suits had been in the store, there would have been countless charred buttons. It became clear that Johns had removed the stock, then staged the fire so he could claim insurance.

Buttons have identified victims of crimes as well as criminals. In the late 1800s in rural Georgia, Elijah Lambert left his farm on a horse and headed to the county seat where he had been ordered to testify in court against horse thieves. As his wife prepared his only white dress shirt, she sewed on a missing button with black thread because she was out of white.

When Lambert didn't return, his wife couldn't alert anyone since there were no close neighbors, no transportation and no way to leave her small children.

After three months, someone came by and took Mrs. Lambert into town to report her missing husband to the authorities. The sheriff showed her a bundle of clothing taken from a dead man found by the side of the road. Mrs. Lambert identified the clothing as her husband's by the white shirt with the button sewed on with black thread.

During the Battle of San Jacinto in 1836 during the Texas Revolution, a fine gold button on a private soldier's shirt caused his Texan captors to suspect he was an officer or someone important. Their suspicions were confirmed when they entered the prisoners' camp, and the other Mexicans shouted, "El Presidente!" The disguised soldier was Mexican President Santa Ana.

Buttons get credit for creative and heroic endeavors, too. Beatrix Potter felt she needed an excuse to go into a tailor's shop to sketch a tailor at work in order to write *The Tailor of Gloucester.* Tearing a button off her coat gave her the excuse.

Buttons are said to have created the slang name "cops" or "coppers" for policemen after New York City's first uniformed police wore copper buttons. The terms have also been traced to England where police officers under Sir Robert Peel wore uniforms with large copper buttons.

In Colonial days, two brothers moved their families from London to Florida. One had a sawmill and the other a flour mill. Both kept their money in crocks in their closets. When the territory became the United States, the brothers would not forsake loyalty to England and decided to move to Nova Scotia. They were permitted to leave, with the restriction that they take no money with them. The women in the families took the lead out of the cloth-covered buttons on the men's coats and vests and replaced it with gold pieces. The families then had financial security in their new homes.

Samuel and Emily Williston would not have been able to fund the Williston Seminary at Easthampton, Massachusetts, in 1841 if not for a button. That button was worn by an English clergyman who was a guest in their home. Emily noticed the unusual buttons on his cape. England was especially strict about button manufacturing secrets leaving England, and Emily saw her chance to learn one of their secrets. When the guest went to bed that night, Emily cut off one of his coat buttons and dismantled it to learn how it was made. Then she remade the button, working far into the night, and put it back on the coat.

She used her wedding gown to make duplicate buttons and soon was selling so many of them that she employed five women to help her. The number of workers grew to 1000, and Emily and Samuel amassed a fortune.

Because Samuel had to walk 100 miles to find a secondary education when he was a young man, the Willistons made a secondary school available in central western Massachusetts. The Williston Seminary opened in 1841.

A brass Yellow Cab Company uniform button from a flea-market garbage pile changed the life of M. W. "Freddie" Speights from Texas. In bankruptcy proceedings at the time in 1969, Freddie sold the button for a nickel. He went back to the trash pile and found a couple more which he sold for a dime each. Over the following months, he dug about 2,000 buttons out of the ground surrounding the trash and sold them for a quarter apiece. These sales lead to a successful career in antique button dealing.

Buttons have brought humor, suspense, romance and boredom into our daily lives. The Reverend Arnold Stilwell told his local Kiwanis Club that he knew a preacher who timed his sermons by putting a candy Lifesaver in his mouth and closed his talk when the Lifesaver dissolved. Once his sermon ran more than thirty minutes when he accidentally put a button in his mouth instead of a Lifesaver.

A famed concert pianist was asked if he felt lonely during a tour of one-nighters. "Not at all," he replied. "After each concert, people line up backstage to congratulate me," he said. "When I see an attractive lady in the line, I rip a button off my vest. Then when she congratulates me, I modestly say, 'What good is it all? I don't even have someone to sew on this button.' Invariably she volunteers and stays."

A female Elvis Presley fan in Norfolk, Virginia, wound up with a button ripped from Presley's shirt when the singer was mobbed at Durham, North Carolina. She ran a classified advertisement offering the button for sale in a Norfolk newspaper. During the night after the ad ran, she received more than 100 phone calls. Offers were as high as $600. The woman took her phone off the hook and decided to keep the button.

A woman in Vancouver found a diamond in a box of old buttons she acquired from the Salvation Army thrift store. When she tried to sell it for $3,000 at a jewelry store, two police officers interceded and tried to take the diamond. The woman, unwilling to relinquish the diamond, swallowed it! She recovered it two days later, and by that time had been cleared by the police.

Al Hattab, a horse who was a 1969 Kentucky Derby contender, loved to eat buttons. In the saddling paddock for a race, he suddenly stripped his groomer's blouse of all buttons. Later, he was being cooled off after a workout. As his young female hot walker (horse groomer who walks horses after a race) was putting him away in his stall, Al Hattab nipped not only the buttons from her shirt, but unhooked her brassiere strap as well. Off came everything, and that gave Al Hattab another first—his first topless hot-walker.

"All because of a button" couldn't apply more aptly to a story than it does for the one told by Angela Clark, English button collector, and her neighbor, Ernie Carver.

Ernie, a twice-widowed gentleman, gave Angela a special button for her collection. The lavender fabric covered button with E embroidered on it had been one of six belonging to Ernie's first wife, Elsie. They were on her blouse on the day in 1940 when she said good-by to Ernie at the London railway station as he went off to fight in World War II. One button came loose from her blouse, and she gave it to him.

Ernie carried the button in his pocket throughout the war years. It stayed with him and continued to offer him comfort after he was taken prisoner. Because of illness and injuries, Ernie was transferred between hospitals and camps all over the Far East long after the war's end. His next of kin at home were informed that Ernie was "Missing—Presumed Dead."

But Ernie was nursed back to health and returned to England where he found an empty space that had once held his home. The entire neighborhood had been bombed during the war. Bulldozers had leveled the ground, and rebuilding had begun. Ernie was informed that his family had perished.

He moved to the country, rebuilt his life as a carpenter and eventually remarried. After his retirement, he lost his second wife and was alone once again when Angela met him.

A couple of years after Angela was given Elsie's button, she gave a button talk to a guild meeting in a village in another county. Members of the guild were told in advance to bring along any special buttons or ones that had stories behind them.

Elsie's button was included in Angela's button display that day. At the conclusion of her talk, Angela was approached by a woman holding something in tissue paper. The woman inquired about Elsie's button and opened her tissue to reveal the five matching buttons which had made up Elsie's set.

The woman said, "My mother has a cold and was not able to come to the meeting today, but she asked me to bring these to show you. These belong to her; she keeps them on her dressing table. They were on a blouse she was wearing the day my father went off to war, and when one of the buttons fell off, she gave it to him. He was killed, and she always hoped the button was in his pocket when he died."

"I think I had better get you a cup of tea," Angela replied. "I've got somebody I think you ought to meet."

Ambiguous Buttons
(Buttons With Double Lives)

Even when buttons are used as clothes fasteners, they often have additional simultaneous uses. They sometimes lead clandestine lives of their own.

They have played the roles of heroes as well as villains. They have served to advertise items, events and people and to designate social, professional and economic rank. They have broadcast deaths in families and nations, as well as romantic alliances. They have disguised all sorts of phenomenal gadgets.

Buttons With Secrets

Buttons with hidden compartments have been used for military, political, domestic, entertainment, sentimental and illegal purposes.

A button with a lethal secret was used in Italy by the Borgias and Medicis as a means of political assassination. It was called the poison button. A tiny vial containing poison was attached to the stud of the button. This deadly vial was concealed in the fold of the assassin's clothing and then brushed against the victim so that the sharp stud scratched his skin. The contents flowed into the abrasion, and the victim fell dead, seemingly from a heart attack.

Buttons containing poison were also made much later in the 1960s. They looked exactly like ordinary Army issue uniform buttons, only they twisted apart so the top could be opened. It's believed that these buttons were issued to special commando outfits, so that the poison could be used in case of capture or torture.

In the 1700s, The Count of Artois wore a set of diamond buttons, each one concealing a miniature watch. King Louis XV also had a set of buttons, each of which was a working watch.

During the American Revolution there was an elderly woman in Philadelphia who served as courier for the American Army while the British were occupying Philadelphia. She traveled to the American camp at Valley Forge or elsewhere carrying nothing that the British troops would see as being suspicious. However, messages were written in the inside of her large coat buttons. The buttons were cut off, the messages read, and the buttons returned to the garments when she went back to the city.

During the Civil War, soldiers concealed gold pieces in their buttons to be used as ransom in case of capture. Buttons were also used to smuggle money when Julia Ellery in Washington, D. C. heard from her husband, Captain Albert Emery, that the Confederate Army was badly in need of financial aid. She covered three dozen gold coins with cloth and attached them down the front of her floor-length traveling dress. She crossed the Potomac River by boat, delivered the coins to Confederate Command Headquarters and returned with the front of her dress unadorned.

Smugglers' buttons were used for smuggling opium, diamonds and pearls and secret messages. Some were screw-apart, dome-shaped types with hollow tops. Japanese artists made such buttons in carved ivory with the joining of the parts completely concealed by the carving. It took a magnifying glass to find the seams.

The Chinese also made smugglers' buttons. Some were in silver with designs such as a dragon on the fronts and Chinese characters hallmarked on the backs. Inside there was an extra silver lining, the center of which was an oval indentation, large enough to hide a potent substance. These buttons were cleverly hinged so that they passed for ordinary buttons. Similar ornate buttons existed as early as the 1600s in Hungary. Some, called "dope peddlers' buttons," had miniature hinges and were manipulated by simply pressing the finger on a small knob to open the button.

There are more modern types of smugglers' buttons. One resembles a paperweight mounted on a metal frame on the front. The reverse side is a metal wire loop shank which turns around to reveal a cavity. Similar types have been used for smuggling drugs like heroin and cocaine.

In the past, prison inmates used to separate two-piece buttons, creating their own secret buttons by hiding tightly-folded bills in them. The prisoners used the bills to buy supplies.

Ambiguous Buttons 15

In World War I, American, Canadian and British soldiers could wear military locket buttons that opened to reveal pictures of their loved ones. Most were shanked with hinges on the sides or tops, but there was one type that had four holes for sewing onto the uniform.

 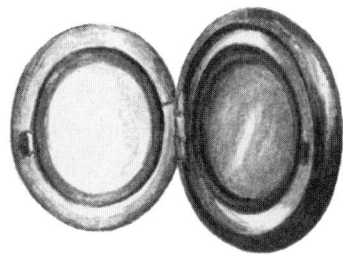

Compass buttons were developed in England and provided by the British, Canadian and American services for airmen in World War II. They looked like regular military buttons of less than a quarter of an inch in diameter, except they contained real compasses. They saved many lives when paratroopers and pilots were forced down in unknown territory. Some were magnetized and sewn into the men's trousers.

There were four different types of compass buttons: metal that hinged or screwed, with no lines of opening showing; metal with compass markings on the backs that didn't open; two-piece where both sides were sewn on separately to form the compass, one side having a tiny center spike and the other side having the markings on the rim; and plastic with compass markings on the backs.

The existence of these compass buttons was kept a secret during the war, and not even other members of the military knew of them. However, the Nazis eventually learned the secret, and they began to examine the buttons on prisoners by twisting the shanks. Some of these buttons had reverse threading, so the compasses couldn't be detected by this maneuver.

Another miraculous military button was packed with a piece of very fine silk. Printed on the silk in invisible ink was a map of northern Europe.

For the map to be seen, the one liquid always available to the troops was used—urine!

Miniature cameras called Button Cameras came on the market in the 1880s. They were used primarily by artists and military men in Germany. The cameras were circular plates in round cases of light, thin metal. They fit into button holes and were constructed to look like ordinary buttons. They were suspended from the neck behind a vest, with the lens projected through the buttonhole. To work one, the photographer came to within a few feet of the subject and pulled the shutter cord which hung down behind the vest. A light tick told him that the exposure was complete. He then repeated the process five times, using the same plate. The resulting pictures were about an inch and one-fourth in diameter, quite like buttons themselves.

In the late 1700s and throughout the 1800s, women wore perfume buttons with perfume in them so as not to stain their clothing. The buttons had hollow tops that could be twisted off, providing space to carry a small wad of perfume-soaked cotton. The domes were perforated so that the perfume could escape. Some of these were made of silver and hallmarked as originating about 1780. The fronts were beautiful handpainted miniature portraits on ivory under glass.

A later type in the late 1800s had a design on velvet set in a metal rim. Women put perfume on the velvet instead of on themselves. They would also stitch the perfume-soaked buttons under their beaus' collars as a constant reminder of their presence.

Much later in the 1940s there were brightly colored plastic buttons made as novelty items that held solid perfume and paste rouge. The fronts resembled cameo buttons in high relief, and the secret compartments were created when the tops screwed off the bases.

Buttons with cavities called sewing buttons held a ball of wax in their cavities. The wax was used for waxing thread. These could be worn as buttons, sewn to the lining of a sewing box or hung from chatelaines around the waists of women, along with keys, scissors and other useful trinkets.

There have been modern buttons in the shape of miniature baseballs that carried three tiny dice.

Kikeshi doll buttons came from Japan. They were shaped like little Japanese maidens, and some had heads that unscrewed from the bodies. Others unscrewed from the bottom. Inside were smaller dolls or other objects. These have sometimes been called "pregnant buttons."

A patent was taken out in 1898 for hollow buttons that looked exactly like pill boxes of the time. They were metal and round with straight, deep sides, with either a screw top or a hinged lid. These were used as receptacles for coins, tickets and pills.

In 1882, a British inventor created buttons that simultaneously ventilated and fastened waterproof coats and rubber garments. They were hollow, perforated balls connected with a hollow stem. The stem opened inside the garment, allowing air inside.

In the 1880s, there were lever-operated political buttons that popped a candidate and his running mate into view when their levers were pressed.

Another unusual kind of button with a secret was a jeweled silver filigreed model. This button came apart into nine different segments when the shank unscrewed.

There were metal buttons that screwed together to create a small box-like compartment into which a paper with name and address could be placed. The purpose of these buttons was for personal identification. One such button said on its outside, "Where I Live/See inside." Another message encircling the buttons said, "The Lost Child Identification Co./Chicago," and in the center, "Unscrew for address."

Peep-hole buttons originated around 1900. They were made of silver and shaped like miniature potatoes, complete with eyes. Two of the eyes on each button contained magnifying lenses scarcely larger than a pin head. Looking through these tiny openings one saw bits of paper with pictures and captions printed on them. The scenes inside some of them were "Bermuda, Packing Onions," "Bermuda, Royal Palms" and "Toys and their Makers, Bermuda."

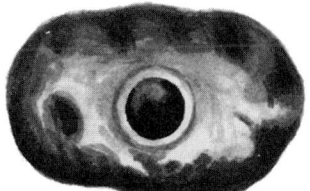

These buttons used Stanhopes, which are small objects with tiny lens paired with pieces of plain glass with a microscopic picture affixed to the glass. The technology was invented by Charles Stanhope, an eccentric English statesman and experimental scientist.

A button with a more obvious "secret" is one that an Ohio woman bought in an antique store that's also a working metal yo-yo. It came with a paper stating it had been a prize in a yo-yo contest.

One other style of secret-compartment button was designed to carry coins for school lunch money or parking meters. The coins look like they are part of the button but in fact can be easily ejected.

Dangerous Uses

In the 1700s, the wearing of buttons made of precious jewels and metals was so common that highway robbers and "footpads" carried razors or knives with which to "bubble" their victims (slash off their buttons.)

In 1765 in France, a rebel leader was the last of his group to be captured by the army in the Prussian Province. At the gate leading to Bohemia, the rebels had fought bravely and desperately until they ran out of ammunition. The leader still had a load of powder left but no bullets. Sitting on the ground, his left leg broken, he ripped a button off his uniform, stuffed it down the barrel of his musket, pulled the trigger and killed the first officer who attempted to seize him.

In the Battle of Carrickfergus in Ireland in 1778, the 62nd Regiment of Foot made a gallant stand in the castle of Carrickfergus against a thousand French troops. When the Regiment ran out of ammunition, the men maintained their defense by firing away their buttons as ammunition balls.

Perfume buttons in the 1880s were made from materials that had an asbestos fiber applied in their manufacture which diffused perfumes. Of course at that time, no one knew asbestos was dangerous.

Brass buttons used to be commonly treated with arsenic to give them a whitish appearance.

In 1893, a woman in England was standing beside a fire when her button made of celluloid burst into flames. Experiments proved that celluloid was very susceptible to heat and readily burned. Cards of vegetable ivory buttons in the 1930s were produced that carried the phrase, "Will Not Burn."

Ohio's pioneer mothers counted the buttons on the clothes of their children at bedtime because the buttons were often made from the seeds of the Nux Vomica plant, a source of deadly strychnine. When one of the buttons was found to be missing, a dose of castor oil was quickly given. The dime-size seeds, satiny in finish and in various colored hues, were fortunately slow to digest.

In 1944, police in Oslo, Norway, removed all the buttons from Vidkun Quisling's clothes to eliminate the possibility of suicide. The former puppet Premier was depressed. It was felt he might break the buttons and use their jagged edges to cut his wrists.

Broken buttons were found among the objects that had been secreted for suicidal purposes by Nazi prisoners of war during World War II.

A button filched a valuable gold watch and chain in the Grand Central Terminal in New York City. The button's owner, after leaving the crowded terminal, discovered the items dangling from his overcoat button.

"Too many buttons to button and unbutton," was a suicide note from a Danish prince, according to Isak Dinasen.

Buttons as Heroes

In addition to saving lives and identifying criminals, buttons also have come to the rescue in more subtle ways.

As early as the 1600s, noblemen had their buttons made of precious metals and studded with jewels. They could flee for their lives, conveniently wearing their wealth.

In the early 1900s when men and women rode in automobiles, buttons were worn from neck to ankle on "dusters" (long, linen coats) to keep the road dirt from ruining their clothing. These buttons had automobile designs on them.

In England during World War I, emotions ran high and were sometimes violently expressed by the public. Any youngish man not in uniform ran the risk of being taunted as a coward. This situation presented a problem for those on war service but not in uniform, such as the non-Naval staff at the Admiralty and Post Office and the Marconi Wireless station operators. To satisfy them, the Admiralty instituted special metal buttons in 1915 with the words, "ON WAR SERVICE," which were worn on blue armbands.

Policemen in the 1930s used to wear buttons with reflector glass centers for night wear.

People in England used "black out" buttons in the 1940s when the country was under heavy bombing from the Germans. The buttons were cloth-covered metal painted with a luminous, phosphorus paint, which made them glow in the dark. They were a safety feature for people who had to be out at night.

In 1967, French authorities issued large reflectorized coat buttons to 25,000 rural children. About 40,000 pedestrians were being struck by cars in France each year, and it was hoped that these buttons would serve as warning signals by making the children more visible.

In 1969, the newest button on the market was called an Emergency Button. It was made of simulated pearl, which looked like a regular shirt button and had a tie-tack type of clutch holder. It went on instantly to replace a lost button and was reusable.

Contemporary buttons save people from fashion mistakes by telling their wearers what kind of accessories can be worn with an outfit and what time of the day, evening or year to wear it. For instance, rhinestone buttons indictate evening wear and fancy accessories, whereas wooden buttons appear on clothing appropriate for daytime wear and casual accessories.

Buttons That Advertise

American businesses have made good use of buttons as advertising mediums over the years. As far back as the mid-1800s, manufacturers were putting their names on pants buttons. All of the overall buttons from the beginning of the twentieth century have advertised manufacturers, trademarks, slogans or names of the companies. Buttons have helped to promote people, as well as to sell products and services. Shank buttons were used for advertising long before the birth of the more modern plastic pinbacks.

Some of the earliest buttons used to advertise were political buttons. The first button to support a cause may have been one found in a colonial site showing a profile of William Pitt, a prominent British spokesman for the opposition in Parliament. The words, "No Stamp Act 1777" were around the top of it.

Every time there was political or social upheaval in America, England or France, buttons appeared that indicated the sentiments of the common man. Witty and malicious sayings were put on buttons to show where the wearer stood on various issues.

The greatest political use of buttons in America has been for presidential elections. Political "button mania" has been around since the 1700s. The first shank buttons to support a president, although they weren't campaign buttons, were created for George Washington's inauguration. One said, "Long Live the President." There were more than twenty others.

Another example of buttons that had political connotations but weren't used as campaign buttons were the teddy bear buttons, in honor of Teddy Roosevelt. In 1909, possum buttons representing William Howard Taft, Roosevelt's political rival, were also produced in numerous designs. The possum was called Billy Possum.

Although the first Andrew Jackson buttons were celebration buttons, the ones worn before his re-election in 1832 were the first campaign buttons. They were worn as normal buttons to fasten clothes, not as the pin-back campaign buttons worn today. Plain gilt buttons were the style then for men, so Jackson's slogan was stamped on the back of the buttons, along with twenty-four stars. This way, the Jackson supporters could wear a dozen or more campaign buttons and still conform to the plain gilt button fashion of the times. They were not unusual in material, size or shape; they followed the current styles.

The campaign buttons for William Henry Harrison in 1836 were the first to use the fronts of the buttons for slogans.

The use of garment campaign buttons reached an all-time high in the Harrison-Van Buren election of 1840 with the Log Cabin and Hard Cider Barrel series. More than fifty varieties of buttons were produced for this campaign. There were three different versions of a log cabin and barrel button supporting Harrison. On one, the cider barrel appeared in front of the cabin to appeal to the hard drinkers. On the second, the barrel stood in the far corner, for moderate drinkers. On the third, the barrel was used as the cabin chimney, for the non-drinkers. Even children's coats were sometimes fastened with Harrison's cider barrel campaign buttons.

In 1842, there was an anti-Van Buren button with a man in a stovepipe thumbing his nose, with a slogan, "You Can't Come in Marty."

In 1876, a button for Tilden said, "No American ever had a greater right to cry, 'I was robbed'," The people had given Tilden a quarter million popular majority; yet he never got to the White House.

There were at least eight campaign buttons made for President Zachary Taylor in 1848. Two show his favorite horse, Old Whitey, whom the rival Democrats said should have been nominated instead of Taylor. On another, the motto "Rough and Ready" appeared. It originated partly from Taylor's carelessness of dress.

Gradually ferrotype or tintype buttons were used for shanked campaign buttons. Instead of engraved likenesses, photos were used, the first showing an unbearded Abraham Lincoln in the 1860 presidential race.

A campaign button poem was printed in a Utica, New York newspaper in May, 1896:

"Though gay is the blossom that sways on the bough,
    As the wind coyly sweeps over the plain,
More brilliant by far are the buttons just now
    That shine in the summer campaign.
And they come by the bushel, the peck or the quart,
    Each brand being shown as the best;
The candidate's glad to supply the best sort—
    And the voter will please do the rest."

Buttons have advertised people's positions on issues other than political ones. John Hancock's coat sported silver buttons with a design of a shepherd shearing his sheep. The motto on the button said, "You gain more by our lives than by our deaths."

People have been known to advertise personal details of their lives through buttons. Lady Caroline Lamb was Lord Byron's first prominent mistress. When Byron jilted her, Lady Caroline made her servants wear buttons with the Latin inscription, "Ne crede Byron" (Do not believe Byron).

Not everyone wants personal details advertised by buttons, however. A doctor's wife bought her husband a set of six buttons with caducei (emblems of the medical profession) on them in the Tender Buttons in New York City. He returned them the following day saying, "I don't want to go around saying . . ." as he repeated six times, emphatically tapping each button as he spoke, ". . . I'm a doctor, I'm a doctor . . . I'm a doctor . . . !"

In 1895 in New York City, the entire "Lord's Prayer" was engraved by an Eaton-Engle Engraving Machine on a tiny pearl button. This engraving was done as an advertising ploy to showcase the fine engraving capabilities of the machine.

Later, buttons advertised everything from metal beds to razors, Buster Brown leggings, Yardley's scents, Heinz 57 pickles and gerkins, Domino cane sugar,

beer, Schenley's whiskey, Premium pork products, wine, boxing gloves and skating rinks. Elsie, the Borden Cow was given in button form to children who patronized stores selling Borden's Ice Cream. Quaker Oats advertised with a medium-sized button that said, "The Grocer's Smile—The Smile That Won't Come Off." Around the figure of a grocer in the center was written, "Quaker Oats."

The Dutchess manufacturing company in Poughkeepsie, N. Y., had as its slogan from 1876 to 1941, "Ten cents a Button, A Dollar A Rip." The saying arose from the company's advertising that Dutchess trousers didn't rip or lose their buttons.

Much later, the Arrow Shirt Company used the phrase to advertise their shirts, "Button for button . . ."

As an advertisement for the free silver movement in 1896, the *Detroit News* offered free German silver buttons the size of a quarter that looked like 25-cent silver pieces to any of its readers. The readers had only to cut the coupon out of the paper and send a silver dime for postage and handling. The Detroit Free Coinage Button Company provided the buttons.

Also in 1896, each package of Sweet Caporal cigarettes contained a celluloid button. Each button depicted a famous actress of the day, national flag, state seal or a famous politician. Collecting these buttons became a fad for boys and girls across the country who strived to complete sets of the various button series.

In the 1930s, celluloid buttons featuring pictures of M G M movie stars were made and marketed on their own to promote stars such as Clark Gable, Tyrone Power, Loretta Young, Robert Taylor, Errol Flynn and Myrna Loy. Plain buttons on cards featuring pictures of popular screen stars were also sold to the public.

In 1937, overcoat buttons were used to advertise Alemite Lubricants for vehicles. On the button fronts they said, "When You Button Up Your Overcoat," and on the backs, "Change to Alemite." Six hundred thousand of them were given away in automobile departments all over the country as part of a campaign designed to make people change from summer to winter lubricant.

In a window of the Emigrant Industrial Bank in New York City, in 1947, a poster read: "Everybody saves buttons. Every home has its stock of buttons. Instinctively we save them because experience has shown how handy they are when the emergency arises. It is just as easy to save 'bucks' as buttons."

Buttons were used in the 1940s as a strong indication of the quality of the garment on which they were sewn. The assumption was that no manufacturer would use cheap buttons on good articles; nor would good buttons be used on worthless articles. Just as a man was judged by the company he kept, so was a garment judged by its buttons.

In the early 1950s, Guinness, the British brewing company, gave landlords sets of six buttons depicting John Gilroy's zoo-keeper and his animals, to wear at their bars to advertise their product. The designs came from advertisements created by the British artist, John Gilroy, with the slogan, "My Goodness—My Guinness," in which a zoo-keeper was seen chasing his charges who had stolen his glass of Guinness.

The Obscure Leonid Hambro Fan Club, made up of piano students at the Juilliard School of Music, tried to increase the club's membership in 1967 by offering a "Keep Leonid Hambro Obscure" button along with a newsletter on the club's activities. For free buttons, people could write to the club. (They refused to tell what Mr. Hambro did, claiming that information would make him less obscure.)

An example of buttons promoting two things at once was a full-page advertisement in a 1993 issue of the *Akron Beacon Journal*. It displayed a four-inch button in the center of an almost blank page. The headline at the top of the page read, "Thanks to 1,124,368 buttons, you can now get more choices in home equity loans and credit lines."

The bottom of the page read, "What people want today are more choices. Diana Epstein, the owner of Tender Buttons, understands that. Which explains why she offers her customers over a million buttons from which to choose.

"At Bank One, we figured if Diana Epstein could offer so many choices in buttons, why couldn't we do whatever it takes to offer homeowners more choices in home equity? . . . But don't thank us for offering homeowners so many choices in home equity. We got the idea the day we met Diana Epstein. And over one million of her buttons."

Buttons as Symbols

Buttons have long been symbols of wealth and position as well as oppression. They've been specifically used to represent a person's rank in life, membership in organizations, place of employment and loyalty to causes. They have been closely associated with both celebrations and mourning practices. In the days of ancient Egypt, China, Assyria, Greece and Rome when buttons were primarily ornamental rather than functional, the buttons served the purpose of distinguishing the rank or office of their wearers.

In the Ming dynasty in the 1600s, large jade buttons were worn on official robes. The emblems (bird, pheasant, stork, tiger, etc.) on these buttons reflected the wearers' ranks.

The Chinese also wore sets of five buttons to fasten their robes. The buttons represented the five virtues of Confucius: kindness, uprightness, decorum, truth and wisdom.

In the 1100s in France, buttons became status symbols of the day. The French Court wore garments button-trimmed from the necklines to the toes.

In the 1500s, class distinction was achieved by using crystal buttons. In the latter part of the century, the commoners began using them too, so the gentry changed to elegant covered buttons of silk, and silver and gold metallic threads.

Charles Dickens said of the diamond buttons of Prince Esterhazy: ". . . the worth of the diamond buttons of that prince represented not only a weight of gold, but of influence, a position of social leadership, a power of obtaining all such good things as he might desire, a modernized version of Aladdin's lamp, that place him very high up in the scale of social demigods."

Fantastic buttons in the 1700s were used by men of the nobility to capture the attention of other members of the court, especially the women. They became walking picture galleries. A man's preferences for amusement were reflected on his buttons, such as card playing, riding horseback, hunting or even his sexual conquests.

Beginning in the mid-1700s and through the early 1900s, household servants of wealthy families wore livery buttons to show what family they represented. The buttons were symbols of status and dignity, as well as identity. They were very fashionable in the 1800s and still exist among the nobility.

Livery button from the John Jacob Astor Family

Status or rank of the family was indicated by the coronet that appeared above the crest. Livery buttons showed when the head of the household was a husbandless British lady because a "lozenge" instead of a shield was used. A widow's lozenge was as personal as her marriage certificate. It bore her family arms, combined with her deceased husband's. When she died, the design could no longer be used by anyone. Occupation was also indicated by a "cap of dignity" on the livery buttons.

Livery button representing an unmarried woman

Sometimes livery buttons had to be changed in order to represent the proper circumstances. An example of a change in livery buttons was in 1814 when the buttons on the livery of the footman of Marie Louise (wife of Napoleon I) still bore the imperial arms of France. Offensive remarks from Austrians caused her to have the buttons removed and replaced by those bearing her own monogram.

When the head of a household died, the metal buttons always were replaced with black ones or covered with a black surface and worn by the household staff for a designated time. Afterwards they resumed wearing livery buttons displaying the household design.

Until World War I, people in most countries used buttons to signify deaths by the wearing of black "mourning buttons." For the funeral of one officer in the Dorset Militia in England, the church cushions were covered in black cloth, and special buttons were made.

Slightly different from the mourning buttons were the memorial buttons which people in the Victorian period used to remember a loved one. These buttons were made with the loved ones' plaited or woven hair.

In the 1800s, coats for federal officers had their buttons arranged so that even if the insignia of the shoulder straps could not be seen, the rank of the officer could be determined at a glance. All general officers wore double-breasted coats, a major general having nine buttons in each row, placed in threes, and a brigadier general eight buttons placed in pairs. Colonels, lieutenant colonels and majors had only seven buttons in each row placed at equal distances apart. Captains and lieutenants had single-breasted coats with nine buttons with an equal distance between buttons.

In the late 1830s, the buttons worn by the Republic of Texas Army distinguished between enlisted men and officers. Both were emblazoned with the Lone Star; but the enlisted men's were brass, and the officers' were silver or gold-plated.

The thirteen buttons that U. S. Navy sailors wear across the top of their trousers represent the thirteen original states.

The French eagle appears on some British buttons to represent battles the English won against the French.

In the past, the dress code at Harvard mandated that buttons be used to indicate the students' year in school. The coats of the freshman had plain button holes and cuffs without buttons. The sophomores had plain button holes, but the cuffs had buttons. The juniors had frogs (cloth closures) for button holes, except for the button holes on the cuffs. The seniors had frogs for the coats as well as the cuffs.

The Tlingit, Haida and other Indians of the Pacific Northwest had family "crests" which they wore to show their ancestry in much the same way Europeans do. The wearing of each traditional design (usually a bird, animal or supernatural being) was rigidly restricted to the families entitled to it.

After Western traders brought the needed materials to the Indians, the button blanket became a popular garment for formal wear. This ceremonial covering was made from a regular trade blanket by sewing large pearl buttons on it to form the crest.

The size and position of buttons on traditional Dutch costumes were used to indicate the regions where the Dutchmen resided. In some regions the color of a man's buttonhole stitching told whether he was in mourning or not. If they were green, he was; if red, he was not.

Buttons were considered finery and were a sign of wealth for the traditional dress among the Lapps in Northern Scandinavia.

In earlier days in Bavaria, buttons on the clothing of women identified the exact contents of their dowries, including how many cows, towels and other household items they had.

Traditional Middle Eastern clothing was always made in such a way that the colors, embroidery and buttons depicted the group or tribe to which one belonged. For instance, the costumes of Turkish Jews were distinctive for details of design and buttons which were gold balls with centers showing a six-pointed star with coral in the middle.

Parents in the 1800s gave their sons "Freedom Suits" with "Freedom Buttons" on them to symbolize their twenty-first birthdays. The buttons often had a design of seven stars and were made of gilt, silver-plate or gold-plate. Each of the seven stars represented three years, accounting for the twenty-one years.

In World War II, American civilians displayed their patriotism by wearing "V for Victory" buttons and buttons depicting the Liberty Bell, the Capitol Building and other landmarks of freedom. Plastic buttons of flags and stars were also very popular. There were Animal Allies buttons that were symbolic animals of our war allies dramatized on colorful buttons: the roaring British lion, the elegant Chinese dragon, the Koala bear and the boxing Australian kangaroo. Most striking was the blue American eagle, super-imposed on a red and white circled disk.

There were also other buttons in the shape of paper scrolls with words from the Declaration of Independence, the Constitution, the Bill of Rights and Lincoln's Gettysburg Address.

Citizens in other countries have also boasted their patriotism through buttons. The entire first verse and the refrain of the French national anthem, "La Marseillaise," have been embossed on a button that was one and one-eighth inches in diameter.

Patriotic buttons were popular for civilians in France during the French Revolution. These buttons reflected the Revolution events from beginning to end. All the battles, opinions and changes in political structure were documented on the buttons worn by men.

The French changed their political buttons every time political views changed. It was said that people changed their buttons, or they lost their heads.

Ambiguous Buttons

In the 1960s, the African Bantu people used buttons on their bridal garments. The price for each button was four cows, which made them an important status symbol indicating wealth. The buttons were carved from elephant ivory or made from a whelk shell with lead bullets forming the shanks.

Buttons have long been used to represent facial features on dolls and stuffed animals. One of Blumenthal Company's best-selling buttons is a small, black half ball that crafters use for eyes on their creations.

Charles Dickens recognized buttons as keys to character. This is from his digest, *All the Year Round:* "Show me a man's buttons and I will tell you his life and character, and daily going of his wife and daughters if he had any. And if he has not I can tell you this, too, and of what manner of womanhood is his laundress and room-keeper."

Versatile Buttons
(Other Uses)

Buttons are a boon to mankind as fasteners, but it is only one of the many ways they have been used. They have helped to save the environment and have developed entire communities. They have replaced money, jewelry and psychiatrists. They have served to decorate and entertain. They have been history teachers. They have been used for purposes that defy the imagination.

Bizarre Uses

In the first half of the 1600s, the fashion was for women to wear face masks called loups. Some were short loups, allowing the mouth and chin to be seen. These were fastened behind the ears with silk cords. The longer chin-length loups were held in place by glass buttons held between the teeth.

In the late 1800s, an elderly lady in Massachusetts replaced her missing four front teeth with ivory buttons for the sake of economy. She pierced the front of her gold dental plate with a needle and used linen thread to sew on the buttons.

One day the lady needed to see a dentist to have a back tooth extracted. The dentist, wanting to keep the button teeth for display, made her a new set of teeth in exchange for the old set with buttons on it.

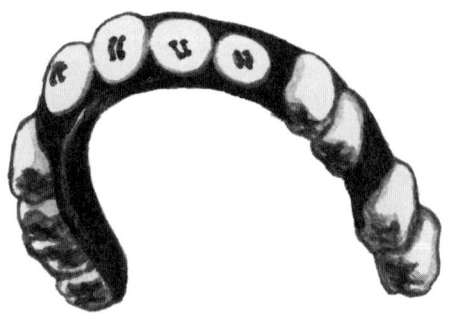

Billy Bob Burns from Texas lost a tooth in Italy in World War II. He found a white celluloid button and carved it into the shape of his missing tooth. The tooth was put into place with dental cement. By the time Billy returned from the War, his celluloid tooth had turned brown but remained intact. In fact, its removal gave the dentist some difficulty.

Buttons have long been used in medical practice. In 1942, a Memphis surgeon used buttons to close abdominal surgery on Leo E. Levy. The buttons were called Murphy Buttons and were first used by John Benjamin Murphy in 1892. They are no longer used but did much to establish the safety of intestinal suture.

Polypropylene surgical buttons have been used in hand surgery and tendon repair so that sutures wouldn't tear the skin. The white buttons, about an inch in diameter, were placed on the skin to hold the suture material beneath the skin in place until the sutures were removed.

In 1973, a woman in Philadelphia had a malignant cyst removed from her lower eyelid. When the bandage was removed, there were four diminutive, two-hole, pearl buttons stitched around her eye. This was to support the tissue. The buttons were removed two weeks after the operation, and there was almost no scarring.

Buttons also have been used for years in veterinary medicine to prevent the sutures from cutting into tissue. One California veterinarian uses buttons from his family's sewing box for this purpose.

In the 1950s, the Duke of Edinburgh chewed buttons, but he didn't swallow them. They were used as an aid to reduce smoking.

Sailors used to cook a silver button with fish to find out if the fish was poisonous. If the button turned black, the fish wasn't safe to eat.

A "Texas Trail Driver" button was used to plug a bullet hole in a hat on display in a Texas museum. The hat had been worn by an old trail driver.

In 1940, Florence Rankin played "America" at the National Button Show on a xylophone made from buttons while an American flag made from red, white and blue buttons was exhibited. The xylophone played an octave and a half in the key of C with a few flats and sharps. A thimble was used for tapping.

Keas, the mountain parrots in New Zealand and popular residents in zoos there, love buttons. If they are unable to carry off the whole garment or cloth to which buttons are attached, they will work diligently to bite off the buttons and fly away with them. Keas are naturally inquisitive about all objects, but buttons intrigue them the most.

A Los Angeles parrot name Syd has always loved buttons, too. He has gone through his owners' closet and chewed off the buttons on their clothes, frequently breaking the buttons. Syd's owners have replaced their buttons at The Button Store and have taken Syd along to pick out buttons of his own. Store owner Omid Hashemi has said, "Syd is my best customer. He's like a kid in a candy store."

Buttons have made tasty treats for various critters. Two types of insects, the larvae of clothes moths and Dermestid beetles, feed upon buttons made of wool, leather, silk, feathers, hair, fur, horn, hoofs and bone.

Casein buttons made newspaper headlines when rats ate them by the thousands as the buttons lay in Liverpool, England, wharf-side warehouses. Casein is a protein substance from milk which is used to make synthetic buttons. In another incident, rats invaded a clothing factory in Stepney, England. They ate all the buttons from finished suits and gobbled up the bags of spare buttons. These buttons were made of a vegetable compound.

Silver-shanked coin buttons were formerly used in Siam for fortune telling. The buttons were fastened to silver chains which hung loosely from a silver ring. The fortune teller tossed the ring to the ground and read predictions based on how the parts fell.

Buttons for Decoration

Buttons as decorations were used as far back as the Bronze Age. The earliest decorative buttons found are from around 2000 BCE. They were seashells carved into shapes and pierced with two holes. These early buttons were ornaments, seals and badges, rather than fasteners. The task of fastening clothing was left to thorns and thongs and later to ties, pins, brooches, buckles and girdles.

The Egyptians wore the first jeweled buttons 4000 years ago as ornaments on their clothes, neck-pieces and armbands.

The early Greeks and Romans used buttons to decorate their loose, free-flowing clothes. A button sometimes served to gather up the material on one shoulder. When people advanced to the stage of writing, the shoulder button was used as a seal to identify the writer.

According to *The Great North Road, A Journey in History* by Frank Morley, Caesar's breastplate may have been decorated, not with real pearls, but with mother-of-pearl buttons.

In the 1100s, the French Court went "button crazy." Some garments were button-trimmed from the neckline to the wearer's toes. During the reign of Philip II, women usually wore fifty buttons on their dresses and men wore seventy-five with twenty on each sleeve.

Western Europe fastened buttons for the first time around the 1200s when clothing styles became more form-fitting. Even then, buttons were mainly decorative pieces of jewelry.

In the 1300s, a woman's cloak might still have had fifty buttons and a man's doublet nearly eighty, essentially as ornaments.

After the evolution of loops, lacings and eventually the buttonhole, buttons still were used extensively as decorations. The effigy of Jon Brandon, who died in 1364, shows forty buttons on the sleeves from the cuffs to the elbows. Buttons were sewn on gloves as ornaments as well as fasteners as early as the 1300s.

The fashion of buttons was taken to decorative extremes during the 1500s. Buttons in gold and silver set with gems were used in rows as ornaments above the cuffs or pockets or anywhere there was an excuse for adornment.

Class distinction was achieved by the fad of using crystal buttons on doublets and waistcoats, still only for ornamentation. Sometimes the tabs were edged with buttons, and often buttons were part of the sleeve and front decorations. Dutchmen's breeches were trimmed with cloth-covered or silver buttons along the outside seam. Mary Queen of Scots had eighty enameled buttons, each set with pearl, trimming one gown. The kings of France and England vied for the most buttons decorating a costume. Henry VIII even wore jeweled buttons under the edge of his hats.

Doctors of physics wore cassocks with long rows of gold buttons as embellishments only. The cassocks were never fastened with the buttons.

Buttons became more of an decoration than ever in the 1600s. They were the only form of jewelry socially permissible for gentlemen. Rulers throughout the world spent fortunes on buttons to decorate their clothes. Jacket buttons were rarely intended to be fastened, but rather to be displayed as status symbols. In the early part of the century, buttons were often present in great numbers and would sometimes start at the neckline and continue down the front of the dress, so close they almost touched, finishing at the hemline. These were not used in a functional way but purely as decoration.

In Renaissance England, Queen Elizabeth I used buttons to fasten and decorate her hundreds of pairs of gloves.

At the court of Charles I of England, even handkerchiefs were decorated with buttons. The handkerchiefs were very small (three-four inches square) and were decorated with names, true love knots and a button at each corner plus one in the middle. They were folded in fours so the middle could be seen. "Handkerchief buttons!" was a street cry in London. Another type of handkerchief had buttons suspended from the corner on a string, which was made into a tassel.

Ladies of the court of Charles II decorated their petticoats and overskirts with rows of fancy buttons.

Versatile Buttons

In the 1700s, wearing buttons that didn't button was a sign of wealth. Throughout this century and into the 1800s, men wore gorgeous decorative buttons, thirty-five on their waistcoats and seventeen on their breeches. Even homespun breeches had a row of dime-sized buttons sewed down the side of each leg. Buttons outlined the entire edge of men's coats and were made of gold, silver and precious gems.

Napoleon wore a hat button that was made with the great French crown-diamonds. It was ornamented with twenty-two immense solitaire gemstones and twenty-one small brilliant gemstones valued at over 20,000 talers.

From 1830 to 1860, dresses were often garnished with hundreds of cloth-covered buttons used for trimming as well as fastening. A single costume often displayed several gross of buttons. Trimming buttons used for ornamentation were sometimes made out of straw and called "basket buttons."

In the 1850s, fringes made of small drop buttons were very fashionable for both skirts and dresses.

In 1867, buttons came in countless varieties and in the most peculiar forms. There were comical groups arranged as sleeve buttons. One design was a large fish cut in two, one half on one sleeve and the other half on the other sleeve.

In the late 1870s, large porcelain buttons colorfully decorated with pictures were a fashion innovation. They were not used to fasten but to add interest by trimming a dress. The actual fastenings were usually concealed hooks and eyes.

In 1878, clothes designs were severely plain, the only socially allowable ornaments being buttons. Large, flat ones were worn three on each side of the opening of cloaks, and pockets were trimmed with a single row down the center.

In the latter 1800s, it was again fashionable to trim dresses with buttons from the throat to the hem of the skirt, and also along the pockets and sleeves. They were set in rows of four, five or six, with the distance between buttons not more than one inch.

A novelty for the decoration of sleeves was a silk band with a row of buttons around the arm just above the elbow.

Probably the most remarkable example of buttons used for decoration is by a group of costermongers (Cockney fruit and vegetable street vendors in England) called the Pearly Kings and Queens. They cover their coats, hats, pants, and dresses with pearl buttons arranged in traditional floral or geometrical designs or sometimes solid masses of pearls. A typical pearly suit contains anywhere from 15,000 to 40,000 buttons and can weigh up to Sixty-three pounds. The buttons are usually sewn on individually because the public tends to pull off buttons as souvenirs. Sometimes the Pearlies' children and even their dogs wear pearl-covered costumes.

These lavishly decorated costumes are worn on holidays, at the races and parades and other festive occasions to help the costermongers raise money for charity. It is said that the showmanship began with Henry Croft in the late 1800s when he wore a suit, waistcoat, top hat and stick entirely covered with pearl buttons to a charity carnival. He was the first Pearly King. When he died, 400 Pearlies in full regalia followed his coffin in decorated donkey carts. He is buried in London at Finchley Cemetery, and his tomb features a statue of him in his button-covered suit.

Doreen and Larry Golding, Pearly King and Queen of Old Kent Road

The Pearlies continue to sponsor charity functions dressed in their magnificent pearl-covered attires.

Looking much like an English Pearly King, Salvador Benitez, a man in France known as the "Crazy Man of Marrana," has danced and entertained in one of his twenty-four button-embellished costumes for holiday celebrations whenever there are fanfares or bands. According to the French newspaper, *Samedi,* Salvador has entertained the local scene to incite joy and laughter and to forget the terrible days in World War I before he was liberated by the Allies.

People in many other countries, such as Peru, use buttons to cover their clothes for celebrations and market days. Folk costumes in Spain have gold and silver buttons that dangle from long thread shanks. Women's

Salvador Benitez

traditional headdresses of the Loima-Akha tribe in Thailand are elaborately decorated with buttons, among coins, beads, feathers and tassels.

In some cultures, buttons are so highly regarded that they are worn decoratively on everyday clothing. Women in Sudan wear veils that are embellished with buttons. The Lapps in Northern Scandinavia have traditionally used buttons in purely decorative roles on their belts and headwear. Buttons have been sewn onto hats in India and made into neck-bands in Africa. Mexican charro buttons are worn down the pant legs of gentlemen ranchers in Spain and Mexico and also by the mariaches.

It is said that the 1940s was the time of buttons in the United States. Designers and homemakers put them in the most unexpected places—hats, gloves, purses, belts and handbags, combs and on postcards. They ran around arm holes and dashed across shoulders. They appeared decoratively from neckline to hemline, both on fronts and backs, in rows on jacket sleeves and all around cuffs. There were button bars in department stores. The slogan was, "Let your buttons go to your head—make earrings to match your outfit." Lord and Taylor, a well-known department store in New York City in the 1940s, adverised a copyrighted button baret.

The fad for ornamenting clothes and accessories with buttons has surged every few years. In 1987, it resurged in Paris. In America, the 1980s saw an emergence of button decorations for young people who used them to decorate their pony tails, barrettes, key rings, hair ribbons, shoestrings and tennis shoes. In 1988, the Butterick Pattern Company offered two sweatshirt patterns with several attractive designs using buttons for decoration. The German pattern company, Burda, introduced a button-covered jacket in its 1990 pattern collection. The New York Transit Company in California has sold button-covered shoes.

Buttons today are still used to decorate fashion accessories, including bracelets, necklaces, belts, hatpins, headbands, rings, cuff-links, scarf clips, tie-tacks and brooches.

Buttons were used to decorate more than clothes and accessories from very early times. In the 1200s they were used to decorate books, purses and scabbards. In *Piers Plowman* in 1377, there is mention of a knife with "buttons overgilt" and in Jean Froissart's *Chronicles,* a book is covered with crimson velvet with "ten botons of sylver and gylte."

Ornamental objects covered with buttons were made mostly during the last half of the 1800s. The base on which the buttons were mounted was usually a piece such as a vase, plate, jug, bottle, jewel box, comb and brush holder, match holder or picture frame. The foundation was covered with putty or plaster, and buttons were pushed into it.

One woman in the 1800s made a replica of the historic monument on top of Bunker Hill, measuring twenty-seven inches in height, and covered it completely with buttons.

A doll named Miss Alferetta was once completely covered in buttons (both dress and hat) by her owner in Massachusetts.

In the 1940s, two silver wine glasses were made from silver buttons once worn by Pio Pico, early governor of the California Territory.

Today such pieces are found in museums, historical houses and private collections.

A hint in a women's magazine from the early Victorian period for decorating one's home tastefully was to heap a wall seat high with pillows ornamented with pearl buttons.

People in the East Indies in the early 1800s used silver buttons to decorate the howdahs (seats with canopies) on their elephants' backs for ceremonial occasions in the great processions of Eastern Princes.

This tradition was similar to decorating horses' bridles with buttons or rosettes. Carriage buttons made in matching colored broadcloth were also used on carriages.

The Navajo Indians used buttons extensively on moccasins, tobacco and medicine pouches, in addition to clothes. Often a Navajo woman with lovely silver buttons sewed up and down the sleeves and down the front of her blouse had a large safety pin securing the garment at the neck.

Hilda Wetherill wrote in the *Atlantic* magazine in 1928 from an Indian trading post where she worked, of an Indian brave who had a gorgeous coat made of plush material and adorned with five buttons made of half-dollars on its front, seven or eight dimes on each sleeve, one on each lapel and seven on the slit up the back.

The Navajo Indians used to make coins into buttons by soldering copper or silver loops on the backs of dimes, quarters and half dollars. The buttons were also used as currency and performed dual duty as buttons and as the family's petty cash supply.

Dimes were used around the cuffs; sometimes in three rows and sometimes two rows went up the back of the sleeve to the elbow. There was often a row or two of half dollars down the front of blouses and around the collar. Dimes and quarters were used to trim leather hat bands, and moccasins were fastened with half dollars as often as with fancy buttons. Tobacco pouches were brightened with rows of dimes. Vests had a row of coins down each side, and leather jerkins often had their original store-buttons removed and replaced with coins.

Other Indian nations also used buttons for decoration. In addition to decorating their festive shirts, dance aprons and leggings with pearl buttons, the Northwest Coast Indians decorated blankets for ceremonial occasions. These blankets displayed the inherited crests of those high in rank, and were worn as robes over the shoulders.

Some other Indian nations put buttons to more chilling uses. The Klamath Indians in Oregon covered a belt with 120 metal buttons that were taken off dead soldiers after a massacre of a village in the 1800s. The Plains Indians braided buttons into scalp locks decorating their war clubs.

In the past, the Malayans often decorated their bodies by wearing a button at the end of their noses.

In the 1990s, buttons were used by fiber artists, jewelry designers, multimedia collage artists, textile artists, handmade paper makers, Christmas tree ornament designers and quilt makers. Handmade paper sculpture artist Corinne Friedman says, "Buttons add the quality of a miniature world to my work."

Buttons for Entertainment

For centuries buttons have been one of the most simple and best-loved toys for children. Many of us today can remember the lure of Mom's or Grandma's button box, explored as soon as we were old enough not to swallow the buttons. Babies in the 1800s even teethed on strings of buttons that their mothers tied together, perhaps life's earliest nonfastening use of buttons.

From button box play, there is a natural progression to more complicated games. "Button, Button, Who's Got the Button" may be the most famous. It's a game kindergartners were once taught to introduce them to group play. They group in a circle with one player in the center who asks, "Button, button, who's got the button?" The children make passing motions back and forth with their hands. One of them does have the button and passes it on. The center player has to guess who has the button until he guesses right. Then that player takes the place in the center, and the game continues.

In the past children chanted, "Rich Man, Poor Man, Beggarman, Thief, Doctor, Lawyer, Indian Chief," as they counted off buttons in sequence in this fortune-telling game. Younger children have also liked to count off buttons, much like daisy petals, with "He loves me, he loves me not . . ."

A simple game without a name required that children put buttons in a pile of sawdust, mix them up and flatten the pile in the shape of a pie. Then the pie was cut and divided. The child with the most buttons got a treat. Another version of this had the buttons emptied into a milk pan. Each child selected a kind of button. The one who found the greatest number of buttons alike was the winner.

In another game called Button, childern tossed the buttons up and caught them as they fell. In the 1800s, girls used to shoot buttons out of little red school houses into school yards like the boys shot marbles. "Hide the Button" was an old-fashioned game that has managed to stay around.

The forerunner of the game, Pitching Pennies, was played in England during the latter 1800s, only with buttons. Large, flat, brass buttons called "bangers" were used just as pennies are used in the American game. The button players had a variation called "On the Line," where bangers were lined up and a "nicker," a larger coachman's button, was used to knock off the line as many as possible in one throw.

A more advanced game that boys played in England had them trading buttons much like children trade baseball cards today. The buttons were rated. "Sinkeys" were "one-ers" and were metal buttons with holes for sewing. "Shankeys" had shanks and were either "two'ers" or "three'ers," depend-

Versatile Buttons 43

Button, Button, who's got the button? "game"

ing on size, beauty or uniqueness. "Liveries" were metal buttons from servants' uniforms. They were "three'ers," "four-ers," or five-ers." The best buttons were "six-ers." These were large picture buttons showing sporting events, animals, people, castles, etc.

An all-consuming pastime for American young girls in the 1800s was collecting buttons for their "charm strings." There were many interesting versions of this "game." It was so popular that it became a well-loved and practiced custom until the end of the 1800s.

In the 1930s in Budapest, Hungary, a button game called Gombozas was a rage among school boys. Eleven buttons were arranged on each side of a table in imitation of soccer and American football. A small button in the middle served as the ball, and the goalie button was usually large. Two players took turns "kicking" the ball toward the opponent's goal line, in strict observance of football rules. There was an art to sending the button by pressing down on its edge with a thumbnail. Some boys possessed coveted buttons that were especially swift and maneuverable.

A homemade button toy from many years ago used by children on rainy days was a contraption consisting of a string and a button. The button was wound with the string, with one end of the string held in each thumb. The thumbs were then gently pulled apart, creating a yo-yo effect and a "whirring sound" from the button.

Another pastime using this technique was a trick boys used to play on the outsides of windows at Halloween time. The buttons would be wound on a string in such a manner that it would wind and rewind itself endlessly, making a "zip, zip, zip" sound as it went.

Buttons today are still used for games, if only for bingo, hopscotch and checkers and to fill in for lost Backgammon and Parcheesi pieces. There are even puzzles showing pictures of buttons. The first was made in 1977 by Marie Bartholet Smith and is 500 pieces and 20 inches by 20 inches.

When people get older, their "button play" sometimes turns into button hobbies. Jewelry is made from buttons, and gardening has been done on *top* of buttons. (See *Buttons as Therapy* section in this chapter.) Vases, wreaths, Christmas decorations, greeting cards, picture frames, pictures themselves, centerpiece bouquets, corsages, dollhouses, birdhouses and miniature furniture have all been made from buttons.

One of the favorite pastimes for proper young ladies in the Edwardian Era (1841–1910), was painting on buttons at home. They also applied the technique of pyrography on buttons.

In the 1960s, many people found personal and artistic expression through creating button mosaics. Peter Engler was one of them. His mosaic, "Santa Fe Trail," is ninety-six inches long by thirty-eight inches high. Approximately 25,000 buttons were sewn on a canvas covered with wool velour to illustrate the settling of Kansas.

Harriet Martin, a button collector and graduate of Parsons School of Design in New York, has used modern button pictures such as one called "Eliza

Doolittle As Picasso Might Have Seen Her." It has been displayed at the University of Arizona science library in a show entitled "Button Diversity."

Over the years buttons have provided us with entertaining sayings and scenes, starting with the rebus buttons and risqué buttons of the 1700s. They were popular forms of amusement first in France and then in England and were designed to tax the imagination and provide a topic of conversation.

Rebus buttons formed a riddle consisting of letters, numbers or objects instead of words to express messages. For example, a bumblebee with the number "4" formed the word "before," or the initials "URA" followed by a picture of a deer made a sentence. Some messages were satirical and political, but most were amorous. French courtiers of the 1700s often wore dozens of these puzzler buttons on their coats, often with very erotic messages.

During this period, caricature buttons were the rage in France. Entertaining satirical scenes depicting nobility were popular. One button made in 1789 showing a caricature head was contoured so that in one position it represented a person cursing the French Revolution; when the button was rotated 180 degrees, it took the form of a pro-Revolutionary person.

King Louis XVI of France had the first pornographic locket buttons in the 1700s. They were also worn in his court on dashing young dandies which caused the ladies to blush and avert their eyes. Whole sets depicted in minute detail the most salacious scenes from the loves of Arentino, a 15th century Italian who wrote erotic satire.

Buttons today still add to merriment, as they did in 1993 for Jackie Cole when she was elected Mayor for the Day and performed the opening ceremony for the Malpas Regatta in England. Her chain of office consisted of a "loo chain" (old-fashioned toilet chain) decorated with buttons. Her attendants wore costumes decorated with buttons. One of the festivity's competitions was to guess the number of buttons on the girls' costumes.

Buttons make perfect souvenirs, and they don't take up much room. As early as the 1700s, Europeans made the "Grand Tour," a popular trip for upper class young men to Rome, Venice, Naples and the Greek Isles. They returned often laden with buttons as trip souvenirs.

Armchair travelers can journey around the world by just looking at buttons. New York, London, Paris and Rome can all be "button toured," since there are numerous buttons depicting landmarks of each city. Practically every point of interest in London has been portrayed on buttons, from castles and museums to hospitals and prisons. The Rome tour could start with a pocketful of buttons that are such exact replicas of coins that they are mistaken for genuine coins. There are portraits of Roman emperors from Augustus to Constantine the Great. There are Raphael's Sistine Madonna and Quirinale, the residence of Italian kings. There are ruins of aqueduct arcades and Minerva, goddess of Rome. In France there is the Eiffel Tower, Napoleon's Tomb, pictures from the Louvre, scenes from the French Revolution and legends, Paris l'Opera and other theaters, Arc De Triumph, Paris boroughs, and many historical monuments that have been destroyed.

Domestic Uses

There have been so many uses around the house for buttons that it's a wonder that they actually find their way to fasten clothes.

In the 1800s, people made "sluts" with buttons. Sluts were makeshift candles which could provide enough light at night for reading, although they were somewhat smoky. They were made by threading a pants button with string, winding the string around it, placing it in a small dish, pouring mutton tallow over it and lighting it.

Also in the 1800s, large pairs of buttons were buckled together and used as clasps on belts and wraps.

One button collector tells of having made a collar for his pet goat when he was a boy by linking large, beautiful Pierrot and Pierette buttons made in 1886, to form a solid row.

Buttons are sometimes used to close the end of pillow cases in order to keep the ticking inside. In parts of Europe it has been customary to button the

Versatile Buttons 47

top sheet to the blanket. The buttons used were large, with about five across the top as well as some on the sides.

Button bedspreads were common in the 1940s. Buttons that were donated by friends were arranged and sewn in patterns on fabric spreads.

A button collector in Massachusetts used large, modern coat buttons to make a walkway by setting them like flagstone on large pieces of mosaic in a foundation of cement.

The Iroquois Indians used buttons received from trades with the French and Dutch as offerings that were buried with their dead.

Traditional Mexican hats have chin-straps which are worn under the chin with the ends dangling from a sliding button.

Some of the earliest buttons date from around 500 BCE when they were used by the Persians to fasten their boots.

Figures on ancient vases, statuettes and friezes suggest that Greeks and Romans used buttons instead of buckles on their armor. These buttons fastened the shoulder straps to the cuirass. The buttons had center holes and were held in place by a knotted string or cord. Instead of buttonholes, cords or leather thongs were wrapped around the buttons and tied.

In the 900s, they were used to fasten metal-framed bags. Buttons found in Sicilian graves from the 1100s had been used as shoe fastenings. During the late 1200s in the time of Edward I of England, buttons were used on shoes and gloves. In the 1500s, the wealthy often sported diamond-buttoned hose.

Netsukes were buttons that were fastened to a cord or chain, which was in turn fastened to a pouch called an *inro* on Japanese traditional clothing from the early 1600s to the mid-1800s. Inros were used to carry small things like tobacco, pipes and writing brushes because the kimonos didn't have pockets.

Early Elizabethan sleeves were often fastened by buttons. Sleeve loops or points were then tied to the buttons.

Gloves have been fastened by buttons for centuries. Gloves that buttoned were worn from the last half of the 1800s through the early part of the 1900s. Evening gloves in the 1800s reached nearly to the shoulder, often buttoning all the way. The length of the gloves was measured in numbers of buttons, numbering from one to thirty.

In the 1800s, outer skirts were sometimes raised at regular intervals by buttons to reveal petticoats. There were also elevator buttons used to hold up ladies' long sweeping skirts when they went outside their homes. The elevators were cords that came together and passed through the dress by small openings in the seams, and the buttons secured the cords. The buttons were drawn forward and tied when the dress was to be raised.

For traveling at that time, square veils were generally worn that had a very large button at each corner. When thrown over a bonnet, the veil was kept in place by the buttons. Large buttons were also fastened on the ends of velvet or ribbons, which were tied around the throat and fell in long streamers at the back.

In 1829, King George IV wore a cocked hat described by a lady of the court as "buttoned up with prodigious fine diamonds."
At that time hats were literally "buttoned up," that is, the brim was turned out at the correct angle and held that way by a button looped to the crown of the hat.

In the early 1800s, bands for tying hair for braiding were made of silk elastic threaded through shoe buttons and sewed into a loop. The button fastened the band.

In the latter 1800s, it was not proper for females to carry a purse to church. Instead they carried button handkerchiefs which held coins for the collection plate. These handkerchiefs had little pockets sewn onto them that buttoned closed. The tradition continued through the 1920s when children carried coins in the handkerchief pockets.

Versatile Buttons   49

In the days when women first began to ride bicycles, there were devices that consisted of buttons with shanks that were used to make "breeches" out of skirts. The contraptions called "bicycle leggin' buttons were fastened to the skirts and clipped the hems together between the legs, thus enabling women to ride safely without getting their legs tangled in material.

Shoes, boots and gaiters, as well as leather leggings called spatterdashers and later "spats," used buttons. Shoes had up to twenty-six buttons each and gloves up to thirty-four buttons each.

Socks with buttons called *tabi* on traditional Japanese Geisha costumes made for a snug fit and if worn a size too small, served to make the dancer more aware of the wooden stage beneath her feet.

In the early 1900s, a New York newspaper described a new bathing suit as having a front with fancy buttons down the center pleat to fasten the suit.

Flapper buttons made of cloth with doll faces, often that of Betty Boop, with short hair and cupid lips were worn in the Roaring 20s as a finishing touch for girls' garters, which were worn on the outside of one stocking below the knee.

Buttons were sewed onto children's sock garters and undershirts in the 1930s. The rarest Mickey Mouse button, made of two-piece brass with a tin back, was one of these buttons.

During the 1940s, buttons were used to fasten purses because of the shortages of metal frames and zippers.

In the 1960s, there were purse buttons with shanks that swirled and were sometimes called purse knobs.

Buttons as Therapy

Button collecting and crafting have provided creative, healthy outlets for people and lifted them from depressions. These activities formally started with button charm strings in the 1800s. However, it wasn't until the 1930s when lack of money, lack of metal for zippers, rationing of gasoline for travel and the appearance of plastic buttons, that button collecting became one of the most popular hobbies in the United States. The novelty plastic buttons made people laugh. They even came on gaily printed cards, complete with verses like: "Lady Bug, Lady Bug/Pert and gay/ Bring me luck/ The live-long day." Collecting them was an inexpensive diversion that took people's minds off World War II. Buttons became a widespread antidote for the doldrums, and today collecting them is still a relaxing hobby that combats loneliness and boredom.

In the 1940s, buttons were marketed heavily to use for updating old fashions into new ones. People were uplifted with the "newness" of their clothes. This habit continued to be encouraged. In 1964, Madame Genevieve Dariaux, director of Nina Ricci, told readers in her book that buttons that came on ready-made budget clothes were sometimes rather ugly. A good trick was to buy a set of amusing buttons and use them to add a personal note. In later years, Millicent Safro, owner of Tender Buttons in New York City, sold skull and cross bone buttons to a Hell's Angel, rabbits coming out of a hat to a magician, lions to men named Leo and on one occasion an entire collection of fifty fox buttons to a Mrs. Fox.

Shy people wear fancy buttons to get attention as a way of communicating without speech, according to a psychologist quoted in the *Los Angeles Times*.

Historically, one of the most therapeutic button crafts is that of button gardening—making an entire miniature, landscaped garden using real plants on top of a large button. Button gardens are made by putting small amounts of soil or wet moss on a flat dress or coat button. By using manicure scissors, bits of colored rocks and tiny figures are added to fit into a theme. Then small succulents are planted in the soil. The holes in the buttons provide drainage. These gardens actually grow and are very resilient.

This hobby became a craze in the 1940s during and after World War II. Women made these gardens for servicemen who had been wounded. Then Gray Ladies and Red Cross workers took the gardens to the bedsides in hospitals, along with eye droppers with which to water them. The men loved the little gardens. They raised morale because the gardens gave the men something to care for, as the gardens needed to be watered and cut back. The demand was great—so great that the Art and Skills Department of the Red Cross trained their own personnel in this art because the volunteers couldn't meet the demand.

During the 1950s, button gardens in hospitals were regarded as "button therapy" and an antidote for monotony. A Gray Lady therapist reported that "veterans are going full tilt, and the boys who are able to get out of bed follow her from veteran to veteran and watch her as she helps each one with his button garden."

Constance Alexander, newspaper columnist and radio commentator, writes of childhood days when she was sick and camped on the living room couch with the family's button box. She sifted through the buttons "as though they were a universe of many sized moons," and she loved the family story that each button told. This, too, was a family tradition, as her mother had comforted herself on sick days with the same button box.

Button box therapy

In 1966, an occupational therapist requested information from the National Button Society about how to make button pictures, so that she could use the hobby for her treatment of convalescing people. Button collages in the 1960s were popular as creative outlets. Some of them were done in conjunction with water colors, ink and crayons to add backgrounds. Buttons were sometimes sewn on, two and three deep, to give a dimensional effect.

Florence Dieckmann in Roanoke, Virginia, has been known as "Ms. Button" by the girls at Youth Haven II, a residential program for troubled female adolescents, where she has volunteered her time to teach crafts to the residents. Ms. Dieckmann earned her nickname because of the button crafts she has taught the young women.

There is something soothing about the gentle click and crunch of buttons as they are poured from a jar, something satisfying about a handful of buttons, and about sorting buttons by colors, sizes, shapes and themes. A sentiment of button collectors is that they like the tactile part of buttons, being able to hold a little bit of history. One collector in Canada said, "You can collect stamps, but you can't handle stamps.

In 1989, Bertha Wittlif found this tactile experience provided by buttons to be a greatly effective treatment in her home for disabled children. She was a button collector and had a plastic, life-sized bathtub full of buttons. She sat the children in the tub with the buttons, and even the hyperactive ones sorted and scooped for as long as eight hours at a time. They often remained calm after the "play time."

The now-closed Renaissance Buttons shop in Chicago had a big steamer trunk called the Treasure Chest full of ten-cent buttons. Children played with it and sometimes played *inside* it to give their parents relaxed shopping time. Many other stores use containers full of buttons as baby-sitters, usually on a smaller scale.

Adults, too, can find peace through the soothing touch of buttons. One woman in New York City used to visit the Tender Buttons store there after her weekly psychiatric appointments. She sat for hours handling the buttons and said it was the only place she could go after her therapy sessions. Another Tender Button customer asked for a button to use for meditation purposes, something peaceful. She eventually chose a Japanese Satsuma button.

In the 1800s, Sir Walter Scott told of the confidence that a classmate got from fondling a button on his waistcoat whenever the classmate was called upon to answer a question in class. The boy was at the top of their class academically, so young Walter jealously and secretly removed the button. The next time the boy answered a question, his fingers sought the supportive button, but found it missing. He became distressed and confounded. Walter answered and rose to the top of the class, as the boy had lost his confidence. Later in life, Sir Walter regretted his unkind act.

Buttons as Teachers

Almost everything in history has been recorded in button form. Buttons of the past reflect every art, industry, calling, trade, profession and invention; every bird, fish, insect and animal known and some imagined. They portray history, romance and religion and mirror the styles of yesteryear. They commemorate events, social trends and record social or political upheaval. They give commentary on religious beliefs, games, pets, sports, books, music, painting, fashion, manufacturing and sentiments of the era in which they were made. They honor famous personalities, places and works of art. They give us small glimpses of the great and obscure in history. They are used by scientists and historians to give us accurate information about our ancestors and their accomplishments. Even the button manufacturing process has had an educational effect on the world.

Children's first educational play often has involved the stringing, counting and sorting of buttons according to their shapes, colors and materials. A Wrigley's Spearmint Gum advertisement in a 1957 issue of *Redbook Magazine* showed a little girl engaged in stringing a necklace from buttons. The ad was educational in nature and stressed the hours of instructional benefits that buttons hold for children, as well as the development of concentration, coordination and imagination.

One elementary school teacher puts buttons in a very large carton in her classroom and uses this "button box" for students with too much energy to busy themselves by crawling in and matching buttons by sizes, shapes and colors.

Elementary school teacher and button collector Lorraine Bahr keeps track of the number of buttons she has by having her third grade students count them. She has over 120,000 buttons, so her students get a hands-on experience with the concept of large numbers.

Button collector Willie Marie Hall, a former Sunday School teacher, used her buttons as an aid to help students memorize the Bible books. For each of the sixty-six books, Mrs. Hall had a scripture verse and a button depicting something from that verse. For example, a button with a turtle on it represented the book of Numbers, chapter six, verse ten. The book of Luke was represented by a fan depicting chapter three, verse seventeen.

Numbers 6:10
And on the eighth day he shall bring two turtles, or two young pigeons, to the priest, to the door of the tabernacle of the congregation.

Luke 3:17
Whose fan is in his hand, and he will thoroughly purge his floor, and will gather the wheat into his garner; but the chaff he will burn with fire unquenchable.

The Royal National Institute for the Blind in London sells sets of plastic buttons with sixteen shapes to aid blind people when they dress. Each button shape represents a different color, thereby enabling blind people to identify colors through shapes.

In the 1950s, two button collectors published a booklet entitled *The Button Book From Shakespeare*. In it were cards and quotations from Shakespeare and spaces to mount appropriate buttons. It served as a learning tool for both button collectors and literature students.

Buttons have been especially helpful to archeologists in providing clues while excavating. In the 1950s, a farmer digging in his fields near Genoa, Italy, found two skeletons. By examining the military buttons and insignia, it was learned that the men had been soldiers of Napoleon's army around 1800.

Archaeologists have learned through the excavation of buttons that Old World religious practices were continued by West African slaves long after their arrival in the United States. The buttons, which were usually white, represented the underworld.

In the early 1900s, a small group of men organized the American Buttonists Society with the purpose of supplementing history by evidence from old buttons found on ancient and modern battlefields and campsites. They added much to the existing knowledge of early historical events through their excavations and studies of the many buttons they found. They were especially helpful in tracing numerous events from the American Revolution and the War of 1812.

After two years of searching for the location of Fort Stansbury, headquarters of the Third Regiment, United States Infantry during the Seminole Wars in Florida from 1835–1841, Dr. Stanley Olsen, and his son John found it. in 1963. They initially found an old United States Navy officer's sleeve button, thus identifying the exact location of the fort. Excavators later found many other military buttons and other artifacts.

Scientists at Los Alamos National Laboratory in New Mexico have used brass buttons from the 1860s to determine the amount of carbon dioxide in the atmosphere of that era as contrasted with that of today. They did so by drilling holes in the buttons and studying the escaping air.

Art historians have found buttons to be useful for identifying works of art. One example is a bust which was originally said to be of Oliver H. Perry, who was a United States Navy Officer and hero in the War of 1812. That is now questioned because its coat buttons are similar to those of a Confederate field officer.

Genealogists study buttons bearing family crests to illuminate history. A family's identity can be traced through the crests that appear on livery buttons.

Buttons in the Bank
(The Button Business)

There is much evidence that buttons have been used as currency throughout history beginning as early as the 1500s. Buttons continue to have buying power in many parts of the world where natives accept buttons in their trading deals.

Button-making as a trade started in the 1200s with guilds for French craftsmen which were governed by law, and it has gained momentum ever since. From small home-operated and family-run businesses to huge multi-million dollar companies, buttons and button products have impacted national economies for centuries.

Buttons as Money

Kings and nobility used their gold, silver and jeweled buttons as investments for centuries before the existence of banks. The late 1500s was an age of increasing travel with high risks involved, and the bank of England was still nearly 100 years away. In Elizabethan days, families put all their savings into silver buttons and sewed them onto their Sunday best.

A man with twenty or thirty buttons on his clothing was never "broke," not unless he was "bubbled" (robbed) by a footpad—that is if a thief stole his buttons by slashing them off with a razor or knife carried for that purpose. Thieves found this method much more profitable than stealing the purses of the wealthy.

In England in the 1600s, Queen Henrietta Maria sold King Charles I's diamond buttons to raise money for troops. And King Louis XIV of France sometimes paid his mistresses with buttons of gold embellished with precious stones from his attire.

Buttons in the Bank

A pair of valuable diamond shirt-sleeve buttons were part of the royal treasure sold in Rome to aid the impoverished followers of the Stuart cause in the 1700s.

Metal buttons in England in the 1700s had a certain currency value, for during war, the shanks used to be cut off and the pieces passed as half-pence.

Bullet-shaped silver coins were used in Siam from at least the 1400s to the mid-1800s when the silver was not coined but paid in weight. These were often made into coat and vest buttons and sold by jewelers. The Siamese houseboys, who loved to gamble, wore these bullet-shaped buttons and used them to pay wagers.

Gilded brass buttons known as "trade gilts" were made in America, France and England for the Oriental market. These buttons were traded for porcelains, teas, spices, silks and fans in the Orient. The first American trading voyage using these buttons took place in 1785.

In 1806, an entry was made in the Lewis and Clark expedition journal indicating that members purchased wood and three dogs from Indians in exchange for pewter buttons which they had made. The expedition carried a hand-operated button mold as necessary equipment.

Northwest fur traders in the United States traded buttons for furs from the Indians. In the 1600s, John Elliott ordered three gross of pewter buttons for Indian trading.

Captain Bonneville's Survey, the American Fur Company and the Rocky Mountain Fur Company traded buttons for furs along the Columbia River in the 1830s. In *Captain Bonneville's Adventures,* Washington Irving wrote that on a journey west he purchased a skin for a couple of buttons.

During this period there were also a number of "free or amateur" traders doing button trading with the Indians. One such trader, Nathaniel Wyeth, brought the Phoenix buttons which had been made for the army of King Christophe of Haiti, to the Northwest.

When the Dutch claimed Connecticut, they built a trading post at Hartford where they swapped bone collar buttons with the Indians for beaver and otter skins.

The Dutch also purchased the island of Manhattan from the Indians for the equivalent of $24 in buttons and beads.

In 1838, Timothy Henry Sadler used buttons to bring more money out of England when he immigrated to the United States. His vest buttons were made from four-pence pieces.

When a Navajo Indian came to trading posts for supplies and ran out of money in his pocket, he merely clipped off one of his buttons in exchange for coffee, sugar, jam, etc. Silver buttons or coin buttons were acceptable at any trading post on the reservation. Although there was a very rigid law imposing a penalty for defacing United States money, the authorities decided that the Navajo's money was still legal tender, since there was no mutilation. In fact, the opinion was that he had added value to the coins, in the way of the fastener of silver or copper.

In 1953, however, twenty-nine silver dollar buttons weren't accepted by a Colorado judge from three Indians who were fined for drunkenness. The buttons had come off the clothes of Indians' wives and had been defaced by welded copper loops so they could be attached on clothing. The judge initially agreed to accept them as payment, but the bank refused them.

In the Ozark Mountain region there was a time when pants buttons were used as legal tender or barter. An account of such a business transaction once appeared in the *Ozarks Mountaineer*. An early pioneer cut the buttons off his trousers in a country store and gave them to the clerk to pay the balance on a clock for his wife. Buttons were scarce and valuable at the time. The mountaineer probably used nails or strong thorns from a hawthorn tree to hold his pants up after he parted with his buttons.

Highland men from Scotland used to carry a silver button when venturing into foreign lands after fortune and fame. The button enabled them to be given a decent burial if they died far from home. In wartime, their kilt buttons made of gold and silver had the wearer's name and hometown engraved on the backs. These served as payment for shipping the bodies back home or to nurse the wounded. In Holland also, a gentleman who owned a couple of large solid silver buttons always was assured a proper burial.

Many jokes have been told about people putting buttons instead of money in church collection plates during World War II. One hobby magazine in 1945 said the collecting of old buttons often brought large monetary gains later, and it must have been encouraging for clergymen. There was some truth to the jokes, because during that decade a pastor's wife in Montreal made a silk gown featuring scroll work in buttons to sell at a church fair with buttons that came from the Sunday offerings.

Wives have been bought in the African Pangaw tribe in Tanzania for a hatful of buttons, among other things.

In Switzerland, shopkeepers have said to customers who seem to be short of money, "If you don't have enough money, give me your buttons."

Buttons as Business

The button industry has played a part in the economic life of England since medieval times. The Dorset button industry was started by Abraham Case in the mid-1600s. It became a cottage industry, meaning that the whole family was involved in making the linen thread buttons. However, ninety percent of the women and girls in the north and east of the county did "buttony." They were the elite workers, leaving farmers without the cheap labor they required. Men made buttons, but it was basically a female monopoly. Some made circles from brass wire, others wove the thread onto the wire in various traditional designs, while the younger members of the family sewed the buttons onto cards or papers.

The Dorset button industry flourished, and Dorset was affluent until the Great Exhibition of 1851 when Ashton's Patent Button Machine was introduced. The machine enabled the Dorset-type buttons to be made more quickly and cheaply. This ended the Dorset button industry and caused extreme poverty and near starvation to the workers in Dorset. Many thousands of buttons already made there could not find a market, and within two years the area was destitute. Families had to immigrate to Australia and Canada at the expense of the government and the local land owners. The Case family was forced to find employment with the local gentry.

Handmade Dorset buttons were resurrected briefly around the turn of the 20th century by Lady Elliot Lees of Lytchett, who ran a Christian mission which provided work for women in the area. Profits from this endeavor provided money and help for destitute women. World War I brought an end to this charitable endeavor. The cottage that was used for the project operates today as The Old Button Shop, run by Thelma Johns. In 1934 at the close of the project, all leftover buttons were tucked away in a cottage across the street, belonging to Mrs. Johns' brother and village blacksmith, Peter Tuson. He didn't want the buttons and eventually threw them in his backyard. The second Lady Lees, Lady Madelain, sent someone to get the buttons and took many of them to America where she sold them to finance religious films.

Another Dorset cottage industry made crocheted fabric buttons. They were popular in the 1860s–1900. However, this industry also became a victim of machine-made buttons.

The production of buttons in Birmingham, England, was the major factor behind the prosperity of that town in the 1700s and 1800s. Birmingham used to be known as the button capital of the world, a title it took away from France by working smarter, not harder. The claim was, "The manufacturer of Birmingham was as bold as his buttons and as bright as 'em!" At one time it was said that Birmingham buckled and buttoned the three kingdoms and half the world besides. The poet John Hone said, "It seems here as if God had only created men for making buttons."

It was commonly thought that in the 1800s five shillings was all the money required to start a man in the pearl button trade in Birmingham. A small quantity of shell for a craftsman reaped big profits. Many local fortunes were made, and the City Hall was built on a foundation of the shells from which pearl button blanks were cut.

Birmingham factories made a multitude of other kinds of buttons in addition to pearl ones. Many of the world's new materials and button inventions were the direct result of innovations in Birmingham. The trade directories of the mid-1800s showed 280 button-makers. In 1981, there were only four left.

In 1837, buttons and the death of King William IV of England made a man's fortune in Ireland. An uneducated owner of a cloth shop in Ballinabog wrote an illegible letter to a wholesale house in Dublin. The wholesale house thought he wanted a million black covered buttons and sent them by the truckload. When the truckloads of buttons started arriving, the cloth shop owner couldn't pay for them. However, the King died the next day, and the Dublin house bought back all the buttons at a big premium to satisfy demands for mourning buttons.

The American button business started after the American Revolution. Yankee peddlers carried buttons from town to town in small tin trunks held on their backs by harnesses. They sold pewter and brass buttons that they sometimes made themselves. As they sold the buttons, they bought old kettles and pots from their customers and melted them down to make more buttons. By 1830, the peddlers' stocks were so large that many used wagons. They were miniature department stores on wheels. This continued until stores took their business.

England's counterpart to Yankee peddlers were peddlers called flashmen in the 1700s who traveled on foot in the wild parts of England, buying and reselling buttons and other wares and frequenting farm houses and fairs. They paid money for their merchandise until they established credit. They used this credit until people wouldn't extend any more, at which time the flashmen dropped their connections without paying and formed new ones.

In the 1800s, J. F. Boepple immigrated to the United States from Austria with the intention of starting a fresh water pearl button factory. After a long and diligent search around the New York City area, Mr. Boepple gave up on finding the proper kind of mussel shells from which to make the buttons. He moved to Iowa where he undertook a different profession.

One day while swimming in a river near Muscatine in 1888, his foot struck a sharp object and sustained a cut. The offending object proved to be a mussel shell of the type for which he had been searching. As a result, Mr. Boepple soon began to make fresh water pearl buttons, and Muscatine and the surrounding towns developed into a center for this industry.

In the early 1900s, the Apache leader Geronimo had a "button industry" of his own. He was confined to Fort Sill, Oklahoma, where many tourists came to see him. He sold the buttons off his coat for souvenirs, keeping extra ones in his pocket at all times to replace the ones he sold.

Another small beginning resulted when Sue Louis wanted a new linoleum floor for her kitchen. She hand-painted just enough pearl buttons to pay for the floor and sold them at a shop. The buttons were such a huge success that Sue made more and didn't have much time to spend in her kitchen anymore. Her booming button business grew so large that she had franchises and sales representatives all over the country.

JHB Imports also had a humble beginning. In the 1960s, founder Jean Barr traveled to Europe and brought back about 100 unusual buttons. The Denver Dry Goods store liked them and became her first customer. She ran a one-woman operation in her basement for the first few years, traveling to Europe to replenish her button supply. After she put out a catalog her business boomed, and she hired ten women employees who operated their schedules around their families. JHB International Imports is one of today's largest button suppliers.

One of the most heart-warming button-maker stories is that of George E. Schmidt. He had been a hard-working man all his life, compensating for a childhood accident that caused the loss of most of his thumb and first two fingers of his right hand.

Retirement at age seventy-two depressed him, so his daughter asked him to make her some wood buttons in order to cheer him. The result was a button woodworking talent that produced exquisite one-of-a kind studio buttons that landed in prestigious button collections, an exhibit at the Cooper-Hewitt Museum in New York and a reputation as a fine American folk artist. One collector considered him to be the "Grandpa Moses" of studio button designers. (Studio buttons are buttons made especially for the button-collectors' market.)

Buttons in the Bank

Brooks Buttons became well known in England when the Queen allowed young Prince Charles and Princess Anne to accept a set of them. They were allowed to have them because the Brooks Buttons' story was unique. Alan Brooks had been crippled by polio at age three and lost use of his legs. At age twelve he refused an operation to amputate his legs. Instead he used a wheelchair and attended art school. As a hobby he painted buttons as gifts for friends. He married an embroidery artist who had to give up her work due to ill health. They went into the hand-painted studio button business, and their buttons became very collectible before they were forced to give up their work in 1986 and retire to a nursing home.

Perhaps the most inspirational commercial button story is about the town of Gablonz, Czechoslovakia. After World War II, 30,000 Gablonz residents were forced to move across Europe. Most were glass makers and craftsmen, and the town had been France's sole provider for certain types of glass buttons. They formed a new settlement after their migration called Newgablonz, which became world-famous for manufacturing buttons and jewelry.

A contemporary button business, Battersea Buttons, started because it was a personal dream of the company's president. From 1977–1979 Battersea made beautiful pewter buttons, some of which had a patented tiny face molded right on the shanks. One of these faces belonged to the president. Battersea produces custom-made buttons for corporate use and for cities. The buttons are called "City Scapes."

(back)　　　　　　　　　(front)

Battersea Button

Buttons became so commercially popular that a California yarn company accidentally became a button company. Blue Moon Button Art began as a yarn distributor in 1987 with buttons as a mere sideline to compliment their yarns. However, the buttons were more in demand than the yarns, and by the mid-1990s, Blue Moon had over 1200 button designs.

The most successful contemporary commercial development of buttons has taken place in Qiaotou, China. In the 1970s, this community had one hotel, one restaurant and one bus line. In 1987 there were fifty-five hotels, forty-five restaurants and more than thirty bus lines—all because of 900 button factories! In 1993 the factories produced about twelve billion buttons. Rice paddies turned into factory districts and peasants into tycoons. Qiaotou has become the new button capital of the world.

Many of the gains made in the plastics industry are directly attributed to button makers. The button molders were the pioneers, both in material and in end-product design. A *New York Times* article describes how the men's dress-shirt industry scrambled to invent a more durable button. The industry had received a growing number of complaints about buttons breaking or crumbling. Research was conducted on buttons, and companies invented new compounds. The Arrow Company spent more than $300,000 to develop a more resilient button. A team of seven scientists tested the winning button in extremely hot steam presses, dunked them in high concentrations of dry-cleaning solvents and pounded them with weights. The Van Heusen Company tested 100 combinations before settling on one. L. L. Bean devised a "button basher," a two-foot-high metal pipe, to test its buttons.

Joseph Coors, Jr., of the Adolph Coors brewing company read the *New York Times* article and ordered an indestructible button to be made by his ceramics department. In 1993, his research team made one from zirconium oxide which was harder than steel and had two and a half times the strength of steel. It withstood the "drop test" in which a heavy rod fell down a long tube onto the defenseless button. Even though they cost fifteen times the price of the standard shirt button, Nordstrom and several manufacturers of higher-priced men's shirts bought the zirconium buttons.

Buttons lead the way to improved technology in earlier days too. Josiah Wedgwood in England used buttons as trial pieces while he was perfecting his jasper ware. Thomas Boulton designed and made buttons to exploit his new methods with faceted steel. Button makers also perfected a method of silver plating on copper that was called English plate. The valuable process of vulcanizing rubber was discovered by button makers. In New England, brass industries were a direct outcome of the great demand for buttons.

Buttons were used to conserve natural resources in 1990 when Patagonia Inc. and Smith & Hawken formed an agreement with an international conservation group to buy millions of buttons made from the nut of the tagua palm, a tree that grows in the rain forest of northwest Ecuador. The tagua buttons replaced the plastic ones that the companies had used in the past. The objective was to provide a livelihood for people living around a threatened rain forest and to encourage the local population in Ecuador to preserve the rain forest and harvest renewable crops instead of cutting down the trees for logs. Tagua exports from Ecuador were reported to have increased by ten percent as a result of this conservation effort.

Buttons have been involved in businesses in all kinds of small ways. For instance, a single button in each animal's ear is used as a trademark for Steiff stuffed animals. Only when each animal has passed a final quality inspection does it receive its button-in-the-ear symbol. This trademark originally bore an embossed elephant and was introduced in 1904. In 1905, Steiff patented the button and used the name "STEIFF" in block letters instead of the elephant. Later the name of the company was written in cursive script.

Tall Tales About Tiny Buttons
(Button Anecdotes)

Buttons have been involved in events in all parts of the world and in all social and economic levels of society from the White House, courts of kings and Hollywood, to street vendors, poverty-stricken communities and the underworld of crime.

In 1529 Benvenuto Cellini, student of Michelangelo, was commissioned by Pope Clement VII to make the most beautiful and extravagant button ever worn. Cellini spent a year and a half making the gold, six-inch button containing a magnificent diamond and other precious gems. The design showed God the Father and children cherubs in half-relief.

The making of the button was filled with adventure. Cellini endured demands from the Pope two and three times a week to inspect the button's progress. One night the workroom where the button was being made was ransacked, but the priceless jewels and precious metal for the button were concealed from the thief.

Another time the button barely escaped a great flood in Rome. Cellini filled his pockets with the jewels and gave the gold pieces to the ten workmen he employed before they fled the flood.

On one occasion Cellini stayed hidden for eight days after committing a revenge killing. He did nothing during that time but work on the Pope's button.

The famous button was preserved in the Castle of St. Angela after the Pope's death. It was admired for many years by visitors to Rome when it was brought out on Christmas, Easter and St. Peter's days. It has since disappeared, but there is a representation of it in watercolor by F. Bartoli in the British Museum, where it is called a pectoral.

Tall Tales About Tiny Buttons

Pope Clement VII button made by Cellini (Courtesy of the British Museum)

In the 1600s, the Duke of Buckingham wore cloaks and hat bands trimmed with great diamond buttons. He achieved fame because the buttons were so loosely sewn that they consistently fell to the ground. He was immensely popular with the people because the Duke never condescended to stoop and pick up the buttons that dropped.

King George III of England enjoyed button-making so much in the 1700s and early 1800s that he acquired the nickname of "The Royal Button Maker." He used wooden molds, metal facings and cat-gut shanks to produce buttons of the kind then common. It was a very unpopular activity for a king, however. He was widely criticized and caricaturized for it. His detractors used it to symbolize his futility and irresponsibility. Street ballads, doggerel verses and scurrilous pamphlets appeared regarding his fascination with button making. One work was titled "The Button-Maker's Jest Book."

New York Times tells of a chambermaid in 1717 in Leeuwarden, the Netherlands, who was struck with an idea for book designs while slipping pillowcases off pillows. She and her boyfriend made a prototype for a book with buttoned muslin covers on every page. Commercial book makers were not interested in the idea.

A gentleman in New Jersey in the 1700s granted three wishes to his favorite slave. After much thought, the slave decided on the following requests: To remain all his life with his master, to have all the tobacco he could smoke and to have a dressing gown with brass buttons on it.

In 1828, Scoville Manufacturing Company sent two salesmen into Ohio with a load of buttons. Due to the scarcity of cash, the salesmen returned with a half-dozen horses and 395 gallons of whiskey as payment for the buttons.

In the early days in Hawaii after kings died, the custom of the royal family was to have a trusted friend bury the bodies in a secret grave so their enemies couldn't molest them. When King Kamehameha IV died, after reigning from 1855 to 1863, Queen Emma gave his silver buttons to the High Chief Hoopili as part-payment for disposing of the King's remains.

President Zachary Taylor had a reputation for careless dressing. Mrs. Taylor was frequently concerned that his buttons were not fastened tightly. There was apparently cause for her concern, since two of the reproductions of ferrotypes and prints of General Taylor show that there were buttons missing from his coat. He couldn't always keep buttonholes either. He had many wartime near-escapes, and once a bullet entered the breast of his coat, cut through the lining for several inches and came out at the buttonhole, tearing the stitching away.

In the 1800s, a father-in-law chided a young woman for extravagance in the use of so many new buttons on her dress. Her defense was that the button coverings were scraps of fabric too small for pieced quilt work, and the molds were dried peas, which could be salvaged and cooked at a later date.

An elderly woman in the 1800s had managed to obtain print material for a dress and had made it entirely by hand. But she had no buttons for it, nor any money to buy buttons. She had dreamed of wearing it to church the next day,

Tall Tales About Tiny Buttons 69

but of course it was impossible without buttons. Her kind old husband wanted her to have them so badly that he told her he would provide them.

After the soup was eaten that evening, the husband made a set of buttons from the soup bone. They were crude, crooked circles of boiled bone with holes through them, and the backs were very rough from the ridges left from the marrow. But they were buttons, and his wife wore her new dress to church.

There was another couple in the 1800s who had been trying to have a baby for ten years. Every time the woman saw a baby, she cried. She was given a present of a piece of material with tiny yellow roses on it to cheer her. She made a dress for herself, and when there was material left over, she made a baby dress. The buttons she used on her dress didn't look right on the baby dress, and she regretted not getting some tiny yellow rosebud buttons from the country peddler when he was there weeks earlier.

The next day her husband disappeared on his horse and returned with the rosebud buttons, having ridden to a town 60 miles away to get them.

Seven months later, the woman gave birth to a baby daughter who wore the dress with the rosebud buttons for her christening.

In 1840 in California, a young girl named Prudencia Higuera Martinez wore brass buttons on her first day of school. The teacher called her "La Cantinera, the daughter of the regiment," because of the brass buttons. A girl classmate offered Prudencia a beautiful black colt for six of the buttons. Prudencia didn't trade.

In the 1800s, button collector Peggy Dean's grandmother had a cleaning girl who stole her button box full of buttons. The girl, while still at work, hid the box in her bosom and continued to work. Every time she leaned over to clean something, the buttons rattled. The grandmother heard the noise, but realizing how desperately the poor girl wanted the buttons, she allowed the girl to keep them.

Young men who attended West Point in the 1800s would often have flirtations with young women who came to visit with their families in the summers. The men gave the objects of their affection memorial bell buttons. One indignant man wrote, after a failed romance:

> "How you smile away sets of brass buttons.
> Which you wear as your 'Trophies of War';
> Then say, when you're asked where they came from,
> 'Oh, from Stupid—a terrible bore.'"

Theater-goers of the Gay Nineties saw a musical comedy entitled, "The Star Gazer," in which the actor playing Sandy Hook appeared in a long linen "duster," down the front of which was a row of huge buttons. Each button was a cracker, of the large, old-fashioned variety. During a song, Mr. Hook snapped off the buttons, one by one, and ate them along with the top of his walking stick, which was a banana.

Many years ago an eccentric man named Alastair "Eolach" (a name meaning "well-informed") lived in Skelpick in Sutherland. Alastair collected buttons as well as local gossip. Often Alastair would work for buttons instead of money. He would plait ropes of heather, herd cattle or carry packs in exchange for several big buttons.

Alastair put the gossip he collected into rhymes and roamed the villages telling his rhyming tales. He wore a long coat which had rows and rows of buttons. The rest of his buttons he hoarded at home and carefully counted them out like a miser counting his money.

One evening Alastair went to a friend's house where he had been promised three large buttons for telling some rhyming tales. When he arrived he hung his coat on the back of the door and told his stories. When he received the buttons for payment, he noticed something familiar about them. On the way home he discovered that there were three buttons of the same kind missing from his coat. Alastair never visited that house again.

When he was a small boy, Lodoscia Trost's father loved to "shoot" marbles. It seemed he never won, though. One day, after losing his "pennyworth" of marbles, he went to the attic and took one of the perfectly round, black buttons off his sister's coat. Alas, he lost it immediately in the game. After numerous trips to the attic, he had lost all his sister's coat buttons. When she went to get her coat in the fall, Lodoscia's father was in complete disgrace.

Lodoscia is a button collector who inherited the famous six daguerreotype buttons that were the basis for the charming book, *Matilda's Buttons* by Mabel Leigh Hunt. From Lodoscia we learn that Mary Trost, original owner of the buttons, died of typhoid fever at the age of 16, unlike Matilda in the book. The buttons had never been worn, because Mary was too much of a tomboy.

Prior to 1910, ships in Holland had gears made of very hard wood. Sometimes the gears broke. Sailors in their spare time carved buttons as round as possible from the gears' teeth. Then they strung the buttons, anchored the string and threw the buttons overboard where they stayed for at least a month. The friction of the water served as a polisher. When the boats docked, people rushed down to the dock to get these buttons.

In the early 1900s in Kansas City, Missouri, the Santa Fe railroad station was at the end of the street car line. Trainsmen were in the habit of taking the street car and jumping off early to get to the railroad station. One winter day when the ground was covered with sleet, a young trainman prepared to make his usual early jump when the street car conductor warned him of the icy hazard. The young man gave the conductor a scornful look, pulled his coat flap back to show his brass uniform buttons and bragged, "See them Santa Fe buttons!" He jumped off, hitting the ice on his hind end, then shoulder and head. His suitcase and cap went flying. The street car conductor shouted, "What *about* them Santa Fe buttons?"

Buttons can get the plague if they are made of tin. When this button disease occurs, it spreads rapidly and infects all tin articles in its vicinity. The last known epidemic was in Leningrad after the turn of the twentieth century. Some military buttons for soldiers' uniforms were stored away in a cupboard. Suddenly a suspicious-looking rash appeared on them and soon all the buttons were covered with dark spots. The buttons all crumbled and disintegrated before people's eyes, leaving little heaps of gray powder.

Scientists racked their brains trying to find the cause of the strange disease. They finally concluded that the buttons had caught cold! Tin cannot withstand extreme cold. It has two forms—solid metal and powder. The solid metal can turn to powder at temperatures under four degrees below zero if the infection is present.

Manufacturers of certain kinds of buttons were greatly affected by the Volstead Prohibition Act of 1919 because they used beer to make their buttons. The spent yeast that collected from breweries and distilleries was put through a process that turned it into a powder that was hot-pressed into buttons.

During World War I, an industrialist-philanthropist organized an activity for a cohort of elderly people who were eager to make some contribution to the Allied effort.

The man set aside a corner of his factory and constructed a huge bin filled with buttons of various sizes. Three barrels, designated Large, Medium and Small were set up alongside of the bin. The team of senior citizens sorted the buttons according to size for use on military uniforms of American servicemen, or so they were told.

Day after day, these good-hearted patriots were gratified by sorting buttons and helping to defeat Germany. Lonely souls exchanged gossip and made new friendships, some generating geriatric romances.

Each evening after the volunteers left, two burly factory workers came and emptied the barrels back into the bin.

In 1926, *The Evening News* in Philadelphia reported a scare that went through the city when there was a report that one of the fifty-pound buttons on the morning coat on the statue of William Penn was loose and might fall 550 feet onto a street below. The scare was unfounded though because it was learned that the buttons were cast with the coat and could not be detached.

According to an article in *Hobbies* magazine, even professional baseball players have been impressed with buttons. Roger Cramer, when he played for the Philadelphia Athletics, told in an interview of an incident that involved his famous teammate, pitcher Lefty Grove. Grove, after losing a ballgame, ripped off his shirt from neck to waist using both hands. The buttons flew all over the clubhouse room. That was only the beginning of his temper tantrum. When he finished, the clubhouse was in shambles. But the thing that stuck in Cramer's mind "was the sight of those blameless buttons as victims of misplay."

An article in the *Los Angeles Times* in 1947 relates a story from Marcia Clutter, who claimed to have been visited in the middle of one night by a princess who was composed of buttons. The specter requested that Mrs. Clutter create an image of itself, so Mrs. Clutter immediately ripped the buttons from her husband's pajamas and began the project. People from all over the world who believed in spirits contributed buttons for The Princess. Twenty-five thousand buttons later, Mrs. Clutter toured the country with her button companion as a sideshow. The Princess eventually ended up in a booth called The Button Box in the Los Angles Farmers Market.

Soldiers in World War II saw the "Big Button Man of Formosa." He was chief of the Atayal Tribe and held his office by virtue of a neck-piece made of buttons which hung on his chest. If he lost even one of the buttons on the piece, he also lost his life! The piece was square with eight large buttons sewn in the middle. From this center circle there were sixteen rows of buttons like spokes leading to a square outline of buttons near the edge.

During World War II, American prisoners of war in some German camps were stripped of their uniforms, but prisoners from other countries were allowed to keep wearing theirs. This was learned from an American prisoner of war who collected buttons for his neighbor in Connecticut while imprisoned at Stalag IV B. in Muhlberg, Germany.

Since the American didn't have buttons to trade, he traded cigarette butts for buttons. He brought home to his neighbor ninety-five uniform buttons, seventy-four different kinds, representing seventeen countries.

In her book, *My Thirty Years Backstairs at the White House,* Lillian Rogers Parks indicated that First Lady Bess Truman solved the problem of requests for "something from the White House" by simply sending out for a box of buttons. She let them sit around for awhile in the White House and then sent them to all who wrote for a souvenir.

In 1948, *Time* magazine reported that children in Mentor, Ohio, asked for needles, threads and buttons instead of candy at Halloween trick-or-treating. The supplies were sent to help the people in Mentor's sister city, Suoahti, Finland.

There was a rumor in the 1950s that the Canadian Army put edible buttons on 650 parkas sent to its soldiers in Korea and that the buttons could be made into nutritious soup. The Canadians denied this. One report said that soldiers had tasted the buttons and found them to be awful. A Canadian official said, "That is understandable. They are made of tough plastic."

For the movie, "War and Peace," a Swiss button factory was taken over by the movie makers for two weeks to make buttons for the costumes. It took 90 tailors seven months to sew buttons on the costumes.

In the 1960s, radio station WSAI in Cincinnati, Ohio, sponsored a button contest for an injured football player. The school that delivered the greatest number of buttons to WSAI would win a free WSAI Lilt Dance Party, including disc jockeys and a rock and roll band.

The student body of a school from Richmond, Indiana, delivered a staggering 3,429,954 buttons in a tractor-trailer truck, with Richmond's mayor aboard, and won the contest. The buttons, laid edge to edge, would have reached almost the distance from Richmond to Cincinnati! And Richmond was but one of the thrity-five participating schools.

WSAI later disposed of the buttons by selling a bucket for a buck. Remaining buttons after that were donated to charities. Jim Smith, WSAI Program Director said, "WSAI did not push the panic button!"

In 1970 in the Life Button Company plant in New York's garment district, six button packers were buried under hundreds of thousands of buttons when a set of metal storage shelves collapsed and fell on them. Police and co-workers uncovered the women, three of whom were treated at a hospital for back pains and then released.

Tall Tales About Tiny Buttons 75

Years earlier there was another accident involving fifteen tons of buttons. A truck driver was moving the button cargo on a highway when his truck went out of control and struck a tree. No one was hurt, but hours afterwards people were still helping the driver pick up buttons.

Earlier than that a girl named Ann Watts died in 1860 at a button factory because her crinolined dress got caught in a button-making machine. The machine bored horn buttons at a low work bench in the Messes. W. Guest & Company Button Manufacturers.

In 1974, there was a photo exhibit at Gettysburg College called "Through a Buttonhole." It showed the work of Horace Engle whose photographs from the late 1800s were made by a button camera, a camera designed to be used surreptitiously. Peeking through a buttonhole, the tiny lens spied on the world while the camera was hidden under the coat.

Since button clubs and button shows began, there has been confusion surrounding the collecting of bridle buttons, the decorative buttons that were worn on horses' bridles for so many years. When people hear this type of button verbally advertised at button shows, some come in looking for *bridal* buttons for their wedding dresses and are thoroughly confused when they are shown the huge, masculine-looking buttons for horses.

The Omaha Home for Boys in Omaha, Nebraska, used to call the ladies of the Eastern Star who mended and sewed buttons on their clothing, "The Order of the Missing Button."

A Colorado dairyman attached a string magnet to his cows' nose-rings in order to attract metal that the cows would otherwise eat. Many items were retrieved, including two old uniform buttons, one from a Spanish rifle regiment from the 1880s and the other a German or Austrian pattern possibly from World War I.

A bachelor in New Jersey whose landlady was supposed to mend his clothes, grew tired of finding his shirts always without buttons. Desperate, he pierced the lid of a cocoa tin and sewed it to one of his shirts as a hint. When the shirt was returned, he found the lid still in place and opposite a buttonhole of equal size.

It is said that picking up buttons is good luck. It wasn't so for a young man who once found a five-dollar bill on the street, according to William Feather, a well-known writer. From then on, the man never lifted his eyes when walking. In the course of the years, he accumulated 29,416 buttons, a bent back and a miserly disposition.

Things could have been worse, though. He could have been like Frank Smith, who leaned down to pick up a button, but dropped it quickly because it was attached to the rattles of a rattlesnake!

A man in Seyre, Oklahoma, swallowed two of his wife's pearl buttons in the middle of the night, thinking they were his pills.

There was once a clergyman who collected buttons with devils on them. When asked if he didn't have enough devils in his parish, he said, "Yes, but these on buttons I can frame and hang on the wall where I have complete control of them."

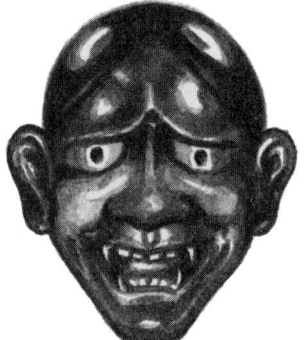

In Penicuik, Scotland, in the 1970s people discovered large amounts of buttons from the Napoleonic period deposited in the ground. During the Napoleonic Wars, captured French soldiers were housed in the local paper mills there. In return for their keep, they had to work. To make the paper, rags had to be mixed with wood pulp, but the buttons had to be removed from the rags first. The buttons were dumped on the land. During World War II, people who lived nearby dug for these buttons and used them because times were hard, but in 1966, new soil was moved to this site, and it's now necessary to dig very deeply to find any buttons.

In 1985, a Yorkshire, England, newspaper reported the discovery of large quantities of buttons by a Jack Russell Terrier named Peggy in her back garden in Ossett. "Peggy started digging a hole and the buttons began pouring out like rain." During two months, Peggy unearthed more than 4,000 old buttons.

The surrounding area used to be a center for the wool and fabric mills, and the buttons were removed from rags before they were reprocessed. The buttons were dumped, even though some were very beautiful, theatrical costume buttons.

In 1979 in London, forty-one-year old George Major earned over 5,000 pounds sterling at a charity event for an organization called BREAK that provided seashore holidays to deprived and handicapped children. He did this by performing with a needle, thread and buttons. For ninety-six hours straight, with little food and no sleep, he decorated a new black velvet suit with more than 22,000 pearl buttons. He was a member of the Pearly Kings and Queens (costermongers), who raise money for hospitals and charities while dressed in costumes covered with pearl buttons.

"Buttons, like chickens, come home to roost," is a slogan Stella McCowen in Ohio has experience to prove. Stella had been collecting buttons for some time and had accumulated 50,000 of them. Then she decided to be a button *collector* instead of an accumulator and spent months sorting a half bushel she didn't want to keep. She gave her daughter many tins and bags of buttons to be sold at a yard sale. They all sold for a few cents apiece.

For about two years those who knew that Stella collected buttons brought batches of them to her saying they had bought the buttons for her at a garage sale. Stella paid for them each time. She was buying back her old buttons!

She sorted again and still had a half bushel of "throwaways." This time she put them in five trash bags and watched while the city crew put them in the garbage truck.

One evening a friend came to Stella's door and said, "Look what Les found at the dump." (Her husband's job was driving a bulldozer at the city landfill.) Stella thanked her nicely, pretending great excitement, knowing full well what was in that box.

A few days later, Stella went for a long drive and put the buttons in a roadside rest area trash container many miles away. She never saw them again.

In Salem, Oregon, the students at Morningside Elementary School decided to make an Indian button blanket as their project for the study of the Northwest Indians. They didn't have any furs to trade for buttons like the Indians did, however. It took them three years to gather enough buttons for the blanket. By that time, the study of Northwest Indians was no longer included in the curriculum. Undaunted, they worked for three months in the

Button blanket, Alex Rasmussen collection, Portland Art Museum (Courtesy Portland Art Museum)

school library, sewing on more than 600 white buttons along the outline of a killer whale, symbol of the Tlingit Tribe of British Columbia.

The blanket was patterned after one displayed in the Indian Room of the Portland Art Museum which has thousands of buttons sewn on a Hudson Bay blanket.

Dalton Stevens, called the Button King of Bishopville, South Carolina, entered his button-covered car in the Artists' Parade of Cars in 1989. The parade was made into a documentary film called "Wild Wheels." *The Houston Post* reported that Stevens' car had 100,000 buttons on it, and that covering things with buttons was his way to amuse himself when Stevens suffered from insomnia.

In 1973, Gerard Walker received a set of Confederate Navy buttons from the 1860s as a gift from a button collector in honor of Gerard's great-grandfather, who helped finance the southern naval fleet. Gerald had the buttons sewn onto a Brooks Brothers blazer to show them off. He wore the blazer for twenty years before a cousin approached him privately at a family party and asked if he were in distressed circumstances because the collar and cuffs on his blazer were beginning to fray.

Gerard's reply was that the blazer was a family heirloom of inestimable value that had been custom-made for his great-grandfather in 1863, and he showed the buttons to prove it.

Mary Agnes, a working mother of the 1990s, overslept one morning. It was bedlam getting her two boys dressed and fed, and to make matters worse, Mary discovered the bottom button was missing from her blouse. She found a proper button and sewed it on.

As she deposited the boys with their baby-sitter, the sitter asked Mary, "Do you know you buttoned your blouse wrong? You have too many buttons on top."

Marilyn Green, who is a button collector, button decorator and author of *The Button Lover's Book,* became hooked on buttons as a child. She learned from her baby book after she wrote her book on buttons, that the first word out of her mouth was "button!"

Buttons can be mesmerizing, as evidenced in the Tender Buttons store in New York City where a woman customer spent the entire day looking at buttons. When she got home that evening, her husband wanted to know where she had been. He, however, did not believe she could have spent the whole day in a *button* shop and called Tender Buttons to verify his wife's story.

Another Tender Buttons customer once brought her dog into the store to buy a button for his coat, and she kept asking him which one he liked. Millicent Safro, store owner, guessed she bought the one which elicited the most tail wagging.

In 1995, Ty Geltmaker drove an urn containing the ashes of his grandmother, Grandma Darling, from Peoria, Illinois, to Marshalltown, Iowa, to bury it alongside his grandpa's grave. Grandma Darling had been a well-known and loved seamstress in Peoria right up to her death at age ninety-nine, she always kept blue bachelor button flowers growing in her yard.

As all the relatives assembled at a motel on the evening before the internment, they were pleasantly shocked to find the Iowa State Button Society's state convention taking place at the motel. Grandma Darling's relatives thought it a most fitting farewell and that she was secretly sewing some of those buttons.

In 1996 in New York, seven-year-old De'Andre Dearinge was suspended from school for five days for sexual harassment after he kissed a girl and ripped a button off her skirt. The boy readily admitted to kissing his classmate because he liked her. As for the button, he said his favorite book was *Corduroy,* a story about a bear with a missing button.

When Todd Brix was a student at Harvard Business School and on his way to an important job interview, he discovered that he was missing a button on his dress shirt. He dashed into a Copymat store, borrowed a jumbo-sized stapler, took the spare button off the lining of his pants, lined it up over the shirt and stapled the button onto the shirt. He didn't get the job, but it wasn't because of a missing button!

Todd complained that buttons frustrate him. "They're all over the place, even in little sewing kits in hotel rooms," he said, "but there are never any instructions that tell how to tie a knot in the thread or what the sewing pattern should be." He believed he would continue to staple them.

Vera in Hemet wrote to Ann Landers that a man on a bus, after being told that his pants' zipper was open, hurried to zip it up. As he did so, the woman seated next to him flipped the tail of her fox fur over her shoulder. The fur got stuck in the man's zipper, and they became hopelessly entangled. Ann Landers' comment was, "That's enough to make a man want to go back to buttons."

In New Haven, Connecticut, lives a tailor named Sidney who doesn't charge for sewing on buttons. When customers bring an item that needs a button, Sidney directs them to a large button box and says, "Find a button that matches, and I'll sew it on free of charge. However, if you like, please put a donation in my charity box."

Once a week a local charity picks up the money in the charity box. In this way Sidney helps his customers, and the customers help the charity.

A fable from many years ago tells about another tailor. One day he made a coat for himself out of very beautiful material, which he wore for years and years. When the coat became threadbare in places, the tailor made a vest out of the parts that weren't worn. He wore it proudly until the front wore thin. Then he made a hat from the back of the vest.

After more years of wear, there were few spots on the hat that weren't worn. But there was enough good material left to make a button, which he did. After awhile the button, too, started to fray around the edges from slipping through a buttonhole so many times.

He threw the button in the wastebasket, but this bothered him. He thought there must be something else to make. He picked the button up and looked at it. "I know," he said. "This button will make a story."

Proper Buttons
(Button Customs)

Buttons have historically been worn by men rather than women. This custom began in the Dark Ages when it was considered to be in bad taste for women to wear buttons. Buttons were considered disgraceful for women in Europe, except for France. Clothes were fastened with buttons and loops; and because these were easy to undo, buttons were construed as proof of loose living. If a woman did happen to wear one, the button was supposed to be kept out of sight. "Pardon me, your button is showing," would have caused her much embarrassment. However, men wore them carved out of hunks of rocks, ranging in size from a walnut to a duck egg. They were worn on the shoulder to gather loosely flowing garments.

Men continued to be the only ones allowed to wear buttons for hundreds of years, except for nobility. When women did begin to wear them, the buttons were usually simple and small and made with material that matched their garments. They were made of wood, bone or tin and were concealed under a fold of cloth to be inconspicuous.

The richest and most elaborate buttons ever made were those of the 1700s, and most of these were worn by gentlemen. It's estimated that before 1820, two thirds of all buttons made were worn by men. Their coats had thirty-five buttons, and breeches were held up with seventeen buttons. Even a homespun pair of breeches would have a row of dime-sized buttons sewed down the side of each leg and three large ones the size of fifty-cent pieces for the front opening. Only a few ladies of rank wore beautiful buttons, and seldom as large or as elaborate as men's buttons. Most women were restricted to hooks or laces and were probably told to keep their lips buttoned about it. Illustrations of gravestones from the 1600s to 1800 show boys with buttons on their jackets and girls with buttonless jackets.

This custom changed in the 1800s when women rebelled against wearing staid clothes and began wearing more ornate fashions. The first two decades of the 1800s were characterized by straight, tubular gowns worn by women. The gowns were held by two drawstrings, one at the neck and the other usually under the bosom. There was little need for buttons until the basque (a tight-fitting bodice) and very full skirt came into fashion in the 1830s.

Women made up for lost button time, beginning in the mid-1800s. In 1865, a newspaper referred to "the button epidemic which had seized upon the ladies of the day."

By 1860, women's dresses and coats flaunted from sixty to 108 buttons per garment, often fancy and ornate. Little girls' dresses had as many as eighty-eight buttons. Boys' outfits were equally well buttoned. Men wore buttons liberally; but by the beginning of the 1900s, their buttons were purely functional.

Well into the 1900, though, women in some countries were still "button abused." In the 1930s, men in India wore large ornamental buttons on the fronts of their coats and six smaller ones on each sleeve. Women there got to wear only inconspicuous, small, four-hole buttons, eight to a blouse.

Button styles and construction have constantly changed throughout history. These changes have been dictated by economics, new materials, methods of manufacturing and the whims of fashion. What was popular in one era was the kiss of fashion death in another. For instance, during the 1600s and 1700s extravagant jeweled buttons were very popular. However in 1830, Lady Howard sent a letter to her sister complaining that a Colonel Cradock had the effrontery to attend an evening reception and create general hostility by wearing a coat with buttons of diamonds and opals.

Many of the seemingly senseless clothing customs surrounding buttons have logical historical and practical explanations.

For instance, the buttons on the sleeves of men's coats are now purely ornamental but once had several practical jobs. When cuff buttons were first used on sleeves, they were a simple and ingenious way of preventing the sleeves from hanging down and impeding movement. Coats were expensive, and the cuffs were the most vulnerable parts to damage. Therefore, they were turned back for protection and buttoned so they wouldn't slip down again.

Another function sleeve buttons had was holding up the ends of coats to protect the fancy lace-trimmed linen shirt cuffs that men wore when they didn't want the cuffs displayed. Of course, the buttons also made it possible to turn back the coat sleeves in order to show off the beautiful shirt cuffs.

An added feature cuff buttons provided was to help men adjust their

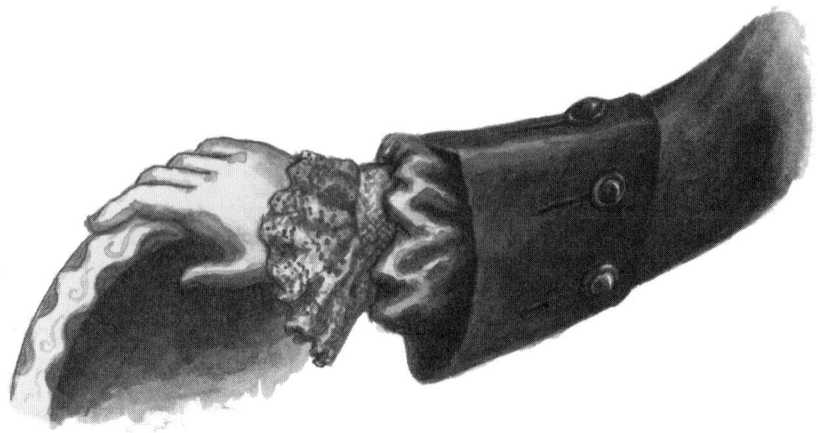

clothes to suit the climate. On cold and windy days, sleeves could be buttoned tightly around the wrist. Another theory is that since gentlemen wore neither mittens nor gloves, they had the sleeves of their coats made long, so that they could draw the sleeves over their hands to the tips of their fingers. The sleeves were made with a slit so that on warm days, they could be turned back to the wrists and buttoned to make cuffs.

Some historians suggest that physicians were the initiators of cuff buttons. Physicians wore their street clothes when making rounds and doing surgery. When they entered a room to perform surgery, they merely unbuttoned their jacket sleeves, rolled them up and proceeded with the surgery.

There is also an earlier, more fundamental reason for the cuff buttons. It is said that Frederick the Great once looked at a sentry in his palace courtyard and saw the shocking sight of the sentry wiping his nose with his sleeve. Three buttons were promptly added to sleeves of every soldier's coat to discourage the unsightly gesture.

Another version of the cuff buttons' origination is that it was Napoleon Bonaparte who, after adding braid to his soldiers' sleeves to break them of their nose-wiping habits to no avail, resorted to having metal buttons sewn around the cuffs.

King George III has also been given credit for starting the custom when he saw one of his men use his sleeve as a handkerchief, which motivated the King to decree the affixing of cuff buttons.

According to other historians, it was Queen Elizabeth I who was responsible for starting the cuff button fashion. In Scotland, however, Queen Charlotte is given the credit for creating the custom to keep men from wiping their mouths with their sleeves.

Edward Wolff, in his book, *Why We Do It,* maintains that buttonholes in lapels once served a useful purpose. In the past, men wore "stand up collars" on their coats. When they went out into the cold, they buttoned their coats up snugly around their throats, using the lapel buttonhole and a "throat button." When they were warm, they opened the upper button for comfort. When they were hot, they turned down their collars around their necks, giving them more freedom and air.

With a single-breasted suit, there was need for only one buttonhole on the left lapel. But with a double-breasted suit that was buttoned from either side, there was need for a buttonhole in each lapel.

Coats with lay-down collars eventually became the style, and throat buttons disappeared, leaving the lapel buttonhole as a reminder of the days when stand-up collars were the vogue.

However, there is another more romantic theory regarding the origination of lapel buttons. When Prince Albert arrived in England in 1840 to marry Queen Victoria, she gave him a tiny bouquet of flowers. The Prince, noted for his charming little courtesies, took a penknife from his pocket, cut a hole in the lapel of his coat and inserted the flowers. This gesture is considered by some to have been the first lapel buttonhole. Prince Albert had his tailor make them in all his suits.

The ornamental buttons at the inside waistlines on the backs of men's dress coats once had utility. They are a hold-over from the days in the 1800s when men wore tail coats and rode horseback. The two little buttons were used to hold up the tails while riding.

An additional use for them may have been to hold sword belts so the belts were even all around. A sagging sword belt detracted greatly from a gentlemen's dignity. Later, when swords were discarded, gentlemen wore coats with flowing skirts. The skirts were considered very fashionable when men were standing still. When men walked, however, the skirts didn't always stay in place. So the skirts were made with a small buttonhole that buttoned them onto the back of the coats.

Another button fashion with a fascinating history that persists today is the custom of men's clothing buttoning from the left to the right and women's from the right to the left.

There are several explanations, and probably all of them contributed to the birth and continuity of this custom. Garments for men and women didn't always button on different sides. Originally, the choice was the tailor's. Fashion historians have traced the origin of men buttoning to the right and women to the left back to the 1400s.

The simplest explanation is that in folklore and superstition, the right side has a masculine significance and the left a feminine one.

There is a theory that all garments originally were fastened from right to left. Most people are right-handed; so it was more convenient to hold the right edge with the left hand, while the right hand was used for inserting the fastener. The direction for men changed when they began carrying swords on a daily basis. Buttoning to the right didn't interfere when drawing a sword from the left side with the right hand because the sword didn't catch on coat openings and edges. Jews and some Protestant groups at one time buttoned their coats right to left to show they did not believe in the violence of swords.

Major Mark Boatner in *Military Customs and Traditions* takes the sword theory a step further by relating that the right side used to be considered the "side of honor" when two people walked together. The reason was because the stronger swordsman walked on the right side so that his sword arm would be unhampered. Pockets weren't in style, so people put their hands into their coat fronts for warmth. When a woman walked with a man, he walked on the side of honor to protect her. A woman's coat buttoned to the left and a man's to the right so both could put their free hands into their coat fronts.

An additional sidewalk buttoning theory is that gentlemen could not peek in the opening between the buttons when they walked on the women's right side when her buttons buttoned from the opposite direction!

Another theory takes the position that men's garments were originally tailored to button from left to right for the convenience of the majority, since most men were right-handed and dressed themselves back then. Most women were right-handed too, but the ones who were wealthy enough to afford the expensive buttons of the day usually had dressing servants. These maids were mostly right-handed, too, and therefore faced the buttons head-on. It was easier to fasten their mistresses' clothes from their right, which was the mistresses' left. Some say that the maid buttoned her mistress from behind, with the lady looking at herself in the mirror, whereas the manservant stood in front of his master and buttoned to the right.

For common women who wore simple buttons, the buttoning from the right to the left could have been because they often carried children in their left arms, leaving their right arms free to do tasks.

Of course, any experienced sales clerk will say that men's and women's clothing button on different sides so they can tell whether to hang a garment on the men's rack or the women's rack!

The placing of buttons just above the knees of boys' short trousers is another survival of a custom that once had a practical use. In the days when grown men wore knee breeches, they displayed their legs to advantage by wearing their trousers very tight. To relieve the strain of the trousers when they were put on and taken off, these garments could be opened at the knee and were equipped with buttons and buttonholes.

Buttons that formed pleats on boys' shirts and pants were both fashionable and functional in Colonial days. As the boys grew, the buttons were unbuttoned, thus lengthening their shirts and pants to accommodate their growing limbs.

Linen shirts became marks of distinction as early as 945 BCE but only the wealthy could afford them. The reason men's vests and coats never button up tightly to the neck is because originally they were cut away to expose the fine linen shirt underneath, which was embellished with ruffles and frills.

Among the many reasons given for men leaving the last buttons of their waistcoats unfastened, the most logical is to prevent the points from curling up. King Edward VII in the early 1900s extended the fashion to vests without the lower buttons. He was one of the best vest busters on record because the lowest buttons on his vests were constantly popping off.

The button-down shirt was first worn by a British polo player. The buttons kept the collar in place and out of the player's face. Brooks Brothers introduced the shirts in the United States in the early 1900s. By the 1920s, the button-down shirt was an accepted part of the business uniform.

During the late 1500s, a custom in Elizabethean England was for women to give their favorite men little handkerchiefs decorated with buttons as tokens

of love. The handkerchiefs were three or four inches square with a button in each corner and one in the center. They were worn by men on their hats or on their breasts. There is a 1659 entry in Samuel Pepys diary saying an old woman sent him a supper and gave him a handkerchief with strawberry buttons on it. One can but speculate whether or not her intentions were romantic.

In the early 1600s under Charles I, the buttoned handkerchief custom continued. However in the mid-1600s, Charles II forbade the imports of the expensive buttons that were used on the handkerchiefs. They continued to be smuggled into England, and men proudly wore their sweetheart's button-adorned handkerchiefs.

Another button custom began in the 1600s and was prevalent in French hunting clubs. The clubs used buttons to officially signify membership. Louis XIV started the custom by giving buttons picturing a stage to those admitted to the Chasse Royale. A person who received one of the buttons from the title holder became a "Button," meaning he was then a member of the club. The button's design later became a hunting one, and a set of them had to be worn on the hunt coat.

Well into the 1800s, Napoleon III and Empress Eugenie continued this tradition. They had frequent hunts with visiting members of the nobility, plus the "Buttons," who were authorized to attend in specially decorated uniforms. The Buttons received from the grand master of the hunt a box containing the number of buttons necessary for the decoration of the uniform and hat. From this custom came the expression, "To have the buttons."

In 1866, an American belle, Lettie Boulton, received a gold button from Napoleon III, himself, at the royal hunting lodge in France. To receive the gold button made her a life member of the Imperial hunts, an honor comparable to receiving a gold medal from the monarch.

In Switzerland, there used to be a tradition that the oldest son in the family inherited the farm, and the oldest daughter inherited the family's button box, handed down from generation to generation.

In the 1800s, it was ill-bred to button gloves while coming through the front door. The buttons had to be completely fastened within the house. Four buttons over the wrist on long gloves allowed the gloves to be slipped back over the hands, but not entirely removed, for afternoon tea, however.

Ball-shaped, crocheted buttons were worn often by French prostitutes. It is speculated that this stopped other Parisians from wearing crocheted buttons.

Buttons on coachmen in the 1800s were made of mother-of-pearl as big as crown pieces. They were enormous because the coachmen were out-of-doors much of the time, and strong gloves and heavy coats were essential parts of their uniforms. They had to be able to manipulate the coat buttons without having to remove their gloves.

For centuries sorrow over deceased loved ones was shown by wearing mourning buttons. As far back as the late 1200s, Henry III made stylish funereal emblems on buttons following the death of his mistress.

In the late 1800s, buttons reflected the different stages of mourning. Full-mourning was one year and one day and required black buttons with a dull finish. Half-mourning was an additional six months and demanded black buttons and allowed part of the finish to shine. Quarter-mourning lasted another three months and permitted the black finish to fully shine.

When Queen Victoria's husband Albert died in 1861, she wore black for the remaining forty years of her life. She particularly wore black jet buttons and decreed her court to do the same. Since the courts set the fashion, black buttons became extremely popular. Most people couldn't afford jet, so they substituted black glass.

It was also proper for the general public to wear mourning buttons in honor of the death of a dignitary. A special mourning button for Ulysses S. Grant was made in 1885 and could be bought on the streets of New York during his great funeral procession. The button's front was covered with black serge of fine quality, crossed by a white silk ribbon on which the word, "Grant" was printed.

When Mary Todd Lincoln didn't honor the deaths of Empress Eugenie or Queen Victoria by wearing mourning buttons, *Godey's Lady's Book,* the ultimate magazine for women's fashions in the 1800s, printed the faux pas.

Black buttons were adopted as tokens of mourning by the Gordon Highlanders who wore them on their gaiters for Sir John Moore, who died in the Battle of La Coruna during the Peninsular War in Spain in 1809.

In the late 1700s there were beautifully made memorial buttons that memorialized deceased loved ones. Usually the initials of the departed were woven into a monogram of fine gold wire and laid against a background of crimson silk or braided hair. A thick crystal was laid over the tip, then set in gold. Sometimes a gold skull and crossbones were added. Other memorial button designs were of hair. The lines of a column, a tower, a ship or a figure, for instance, were constructed of lengths of hair in many colors, and the backgrounds were porcelain.

In the Victorian era, a favorite custom was to use a loved one's hair to make a hair button that was carried as a memorial of that person. These mourning button fashions lasted until the late Victorian Era.

If buttons were given a sinister role by signifying death, they have compensated by being integral parts of celebrations and tokens of love and appreciation.

A custom during the 1800s before the Civil War was for parents to give sons "Freedom Suits" with "Freedom Buttons" on the suits to commemorate their twenty-first birthdays. Until this time the young men were legally required to give their earnings to their fathers. Sometimes the buttons were also called "Coming of Age Buttons."

People have carried pictures of their loved ones, both in and on their buttons. An engaged girl used to give a picture button of herself to her betrothed. Sometimes she snipped off a lock of her hair and framed it in a glass button to be worn near her loved-one's heart.

The tintype button was a fad for men going off to the Civil War. They wore a row of these buttons containing pictures of their loved ones on their waistcoats. Soon the ladies took up the fad and adorned their clothes with full length rows of these buttons. Often they were love tokens. Grooms sometimes wore tintype buttons of their bride on their wedding waistcoats. And fathers wore a set of pictures of their children. There were even "favorite daughter" buttons.

Another romantic button custom is historically associated with West Point cadets. A special removable button at the waist on their full dress jackets is called a "spooney" or "spooner" (sentimental references for flirting or love) button because cadets in past years gave these buttons to their girl friends to commemorate their affection.

Flapper buttons worn by a young woman on her garter in the Roaring 20's were given to a young man to be worn as sleeve holders, announcing that the two were sweethearts.

Button themes were used for social events in the early 1900s. One such event was a button bridal shower given in 1911.

The round cardboard invitations had four holes punched in the center and the writing ran around and around. The room was decorated with strings of colorful cardboard buttons strung on a string. A parasol that had a huge linen button for its top, scattered the shower presents when it was tipped. There were all kinds of buttons, threads, needles, hooks and eyes, scissors and embroidery kits given as gifts.

A round table was covered with a cloth representing a huge button, with the space in the center between the four holes filled with buttons. The table was lit with candles decorated with buttons.

The entertainment consisted of button games, and the refreshments were button themed: sandwiches cut in rounds, cakes baked in rounds, ices molded in rounds, salad garnished with buttons made from slices of beet pickle, and button cakes with jelly between them and with raisins designating the four holes.

Throughout history, buttons have been given as gifts. In 1373, Edward III gave a silver-gilt buttoner with six silver-gilt buttons as a New Year's gift to Phillipa, Chaucer's wife.

Buttons as wedding gifts were quite customary in the 1600s under King Louis' XIV reign. Royalty gave jeweled buttons. The poorer courtiers and citizens gave false gems. Nobles and foreign diplomats seeking favor gave elaborate buttons to the King as gifts. King Louis, himself, gave a bridal gift of sixteen sleeve buttons valued at 12,000 francs in 1698 to Mlle. d'Abigne. Another of his button wedding gifts was to the Regent's daughter when she married the Duke of Modena in 1723. There were nineteen gem-stone buttons worth 35,000 francs.

In 1765, the Infanta Maria Louisa married the future Charles IV of Spain and received six buttons comprising 119 precious and semi-precious stones at the value of 45,000 francs from an aunt as a wedding present.

Many precious buttons have been given to queens over the centuries.

Queen Elizabeth received dozens of buttons made of gold, precious stones, pearl, silk and spangles as new year's gifts. Four dozen buttons of gold, a seed pearl in every one, was one of the these new year's gifts presented in 1557 to Queen Elizabeth by Lady Mary Grey. They were said to be as "big as tablemen or the lesser sort of Sandwich turnips."

An extract from a letter gives the following description of a "small" present given to Queen Elizabeth: "Five dozen gold buttons, shaped like crowns with a flower on top, each set with a pearl and eighteen pairs of gold clasps, and every pair enameled and set with five diamonds and rubies."

Princess Marie Feodorovna, wife of Czar Paul of Russia gave her mother twenty-two buttons in gold frames on which she had penciled miniatures of her beautiful Imperial Palace, Gatchina. The greeting read, "These buttons are presented to the dearest of Mothers by one who is at her feet, humbly beseeching her to accept best wishes and respects for her birthday, today, 25th of June, 1790."

For his first Presidential Inauguration, George Washington gave a set of coat buttons commemorating the event as a gift to each of the delegates. The only other President recorded to give buttons as a gift was President Ronald Reagan, who gave sets of guilded brass blazer buttons to those attending his inauguration. He also gave a limited number of buttons to his staff for his second inauguration.

When General Marquis de Lafayette visited the United States in 1824, the Scovill Manufacturing Company gave him a full set of solid gold coat buttons depicting George Washington as a gift of appreciation for his services to the American colonies. The buttons were made from a single nugget unearthed in North Carolina.

In the 1880s after Lafayette's death, an English governess at the Lafayette chateau found the coat with the presentation buttons on it. When a jeweler pronounced that the buttons were made of solid gold, they were moved into storage with the rest of the General's effects. However, one was kept aside and given as a gift to the governess. The governess moved back to England, married and gave her son the button as a gift on his twenty-first birthday.

The same Lafayette button dies were used again in 1954 to make another solid gold set of buttons which were presented to France, again by the Scovill Manufacturing Company, through Mlle. Genevieve de Galard-Terraube.

After the Sioux outbreak of 1890, the ten Indian chiefs who had remained friendly and persuaded the war party to cease fighting, asked General Miles for something to wear to commemorate the great peace and their part in it. In a short time, a button for each chief arrived from Washington. On the face of these buttons was emblazoned a rising sun, and in the clear sky above were the words, "Peace, Good Will." Below were two clasped hands, on each side of which was a shock of corn and at the bottom was a plow. They were made of silver-plated metal.

At the end of the 1800s, a button was considered an appropriate birthday gift or hostess gift for tea.

When President Harding died in 1923, Mrs. Harding snipped buttons off some of his coats and gave them as mementos, along with sentimental notes, to relatives and admirers.

In the 1940's, the Soviet Union awarded a button to mothers who had ten or more children.

One bygone actress commissioned a button company in California to make plastic buttons preserving her lipsticked kiss marks and sent them to her admirers.

In 1953, as America's gift to Queen Elizabeth II, designer Ceil Chapman was commissioned to reproduce a jeweled button similar to one that might have been worn during the reign of Elizabeth I. Fourteen buttons were made and sewn on a gown designed for the Queen. In addition, a magnificent precious button of gold and enamel set with rubies and diamonds, a modern counterpart of the jeweled buttons worn in the 1500s, was also presented to her. The presentation was made during her Coronation festivities by Miss Chapman as a token of esteem and affection from the women of America.

One button gift never given was to have gone to Jacqueline Kennedy. Vince Hurley, an admiral in the Texas Navy, had a pair of earrings from rare Texas Navy buttons made for her. The buttons matched a set of cufflinks Hurley had previously given to President Kennedy. Hurley had planned to present the earrings on the day before the President was assassinated, but for some reason locked them away instead. Mrs. Kennedy never received them.

A touching button gift-exchange resulted when Peter Jenkins, an officer in the Royal Air Force, ended his four-year United States assignment and exchanged military buttons with an American Air Force buddy. Peter wore the American buttons on his dress uniform for the rest of his military career.

Buttons have been fads off and on throughout history. The 1980s saw a manufacturers' push for a button rage. They decorated pony tail holders and barrettes. One line called "Snapees" featured key rings and other accessories into which buttons snapped. A card of "Wear 'em Anywhere Charmers" in jewelry displays contained twenty-four buttons in a plastic bag stapled to a decorated card showing the buttons on shoes, sweaters and pant legs.

Hallmark once introduced a line of "Friendship Buttons." Their display featured forty-six realistically shaped plastic buttons plus twenty-six letter shaped ones, as well as pencils, hair ribbons, barrettes and shoestrings on which to use the buttons. These buttons were meant to be worn on tennis shoes. There was even a collector's box for favorite buttons. The cards that the buttons came on said, "BUY—TRADE—COLLECT."

Charming Buttons
(Charm Strings and Other Button Strings)

Charm strings or "love strings" were long strings of beautiful buttons, collected individually, by young girls in the last half of the 1800s. These strings were a popular fad mostly among American teenagers in the Eastern states and were intended to be lucky charms that had romantic significance, guaranteeing that the girls would find husbands. As a result of the custom, the Victorian girls who assembled these charm strings became the first major group of button collectors.

The custom of collecting the buttons for charm strings had many superstitions and rituals connected with it. The custom itself was a result of an old European legend that a young girl would find her true love by the time she had strung 1000 buttons to a necklace. One woman was told as a child that if she had a charm string and a crazy quilt, she need never worry about financial security in her old age.

There were many variations of the custom, depending upon locality. In one popular version of the charm string "game," each button had to be a present from someone; and there could be no more than 999 buttons on a string or the owner was doomed to spinsterhood. (Most people knew, however, that this wouldn't be the case, as long as the owner had more charm than the string did! One woman was known to have said, "Land sakes! When George came along, I didn't need the 999th button!")

In one locale, each friend and member of the family had to add the very loveliest button that could be found to the young lady's charm string. Trading, but not buying, was allowed. If duplicates appeared, the owners were criticized. *Accidentally* putting on the 1000th button was to be avoided at all costs.

The 1000th button was the magic one. In some places, adding that 1000th button meant that the young lady was certain to soon meet her "prince charming;" but in other places the day that she received the 1000th button would be the day she would definitely meet her future husband. In another version, the first man who touched the 1000th button was supposed to become the owner's true love. In still another version, the girl would secretly select a button on the string and after adding the 1000th button, would hand the string to suitors. The first one to touch the selected button would be her husband. In one locality, the saying was, "Save 999 buttons on a string, and the next man you see is your husband to be." Elsewhere, custom dictated that the man who *added* the 1000th button would be the prince charming who married the maiden. Sometimes, the girl was expected to steal the 1000th button if she expected to have good luck in finding the right husband!

A grandmotherly woman in the 1940s remembered that when she was a girl, she believed that as soon as her charm string became as long as she was tall she would get married. In a different area, the rule was that the girl had to save the prettiest buttons, all different, in a chain that would measure her mother from head to foot.

The existence of a "touch" button on the charm string was common, although there were variations surrounding the protocol. A touch button was one that the owner of the charm string secretly chose. It was usually an extra-large, fancy button—one that would attract attention on the string. Sometimes the touch button was used to start a young lady's charm string. The most common custom dictated that when someone else looked at the string and touched the touch button, the person would have to give the string's owner a button (or in some locations, two buttons) for her string. However, the custom was sometimes reversed. That is, when a visitor touched the touch button, it was the string owner who had to give the visitor a treasured button.

There were rules that remained consistent, regardless of location, for the assembly of charm strings. No button duplicates were allowed and only buttons with shanks were permitted. Young ladies never bought buttons for their own charm strings—they had to be acquired through grace, from others. The strings were regarded as evidence of the owners' charm, so the temptation to "fudge" a little to bolster one's prestige was great.

Behavior surrounding the collecting of charm string buttons also seemed to have elements of universality. Girls competed with each other to see who would have the prettiest and longest charm string and who would be the first to get 999 buttons. Mothers sometimes started the strings when their daughters were very young.

When the daughters got old enough to do their own collecting, they raided their mothers' and grandmothers' button boxes and appealed to friends and relatives for their finest buttons for charm strings. In New Jersey, girls wound their charm strings around their arms so that each button could be seen and then scoured their neighborhoods with friends, going from door to door begging for more buttons. Neighbors were usually good-natured and brought out the family's button boxes, in which the girls would search for the prettiest buttons. They were often invited to take as many buttons as they wished.

Other good button sources for charm strings were dressmakers and salesmen's button sample cards. When women and girls had dresses made, they bought a few extra buttons to give to their charm string friends. Peddlers in back-country areas would routinely take buttons out of their packs and offer them as gifts to the daughters of the house.

Girls exchanged buttons on birthdays, Christmas and any other time they fancied. In Palmyra, New York, they each kept separate strings of duplicate buttons for trading purposes. In the latter 1800s, girls used to sit on the "horse blocks" in front of their homes and trade buttons.

In some communities, charm strings were brought out when afternoon callers came for tea. The progress of the strings was shown and perhaps a few additions were added by enticing the guests to touch the touch button. Frequently, when charm strings were in the making, girls kept them in plain view and called attention to them with pride when visitors came. The tradition was similar to that of showing picture albums to guests, which became a popular pastime in the 1900s.

As the girls grew into young ladies, it was common for suitors of the charm-string makers to come calling with a handful of different buttons from the dry goods store, hoping to gain favor. It was similar to a box of candy or flowers that might be brought today. The more the young man liked the young woman, the more buttons he brought to get her charm string to 999 buttons quickly. In at least one instance, a young man proposed marriage to his sweetheart by cutting off a button from his shirt, telling her to save it and asking her to put it on her charm string last.

Charm string buttons were made from all types of buttons available in their time period: glass (milk, silver luster, colored, especially black), china, fabric, small metals, picture buttons, horn, papier mâché, Goodyear rubber, vegetable ivory, pearl, brass, kaleidoscopes, reflectors, metal pants buttons, paperweights, gutta percha, Confederate Infantry buttons, campaign buttons and jeweled cameos. The strings were strung with fish wire, shoe thread, ribbons and sometimes chains.

The girls used to restring their charm strings often, but the final arrangement usually reflected artistic merit or a sense of order in some respect. For example, one might have been strung in order of size, another according to color.

Finished charm strings were frequently displayed in the parlor, sometimes coiled around a lamp base or perhaps draping from picture to picture on the wall.

As popular and entertaining as charm strings were, they were not the only kind of button strings. Sometimes the strings were called just "button strings," and the number 999 had no significance except to demonstrate which of one's friends could get to that number first. One button on the string was often the "charm," and if someone guessed it on the first try, the person could select any button on the string.

In some areas of the country, the number of buttons on a string was not limited. It could go on and on, as long as the owner didn't string two of a kind on the same string. If a caller discovered a duplicate, the person was entitled to cut the string and scatter buttons all over the parlor floor. Then the caller took the duplicate button home.

There were "memory strings" where each button was a souvenir of a relative, friend or special occasion. In this case, when young girls went from house to house asking for buttons, they would ask the housewives for "a button to remember them by." These button strings were like "rosaries of memories."

There were button strings that mothers made to keep their babies amused and quiet. Many babies cut their teeth on button strings.

There were military buttons strung together to rekindle stories of early battles.

Other kinds of button strings were carried in early days by peddlers when they drove around the country with a wagon loaded with household goods and notions. The buttons were on long strings and were sold by the half yard, still on the strings.

The button string fad was revived with new energy in 1883 when John Tingue, a wealthy manufacturer in Connecticut, was impressed by a string of 1432 buttons at a fair. Two young ladies said they could easily put 2500 on a string. Mr. Tingue, a philanthropic type, said he would give them $50 if they could do it in thirty days. They brought him a string of 2700 buttons on the 29th day.

Mr. Tingue immediately said he would give another $50 to each of the first three young ladies under twenty years of age to deliver to him strings of 2500 shanked buttons, with no two alike, within thirty days. "The Seymour Record," the local newspaper in Seymour, Connecticut, published Mr. Tingue's offer but left the word "first" out of the "first three young ladies." Many newspapers ran the story, and it caused great excitement from coast to coast. At the contest's end, Mr. Tingue had over thirty strings, totaling over 90,000 buttons and costing him $4000. The heaviest weighed 14 pounds. Attached to one string was a three and one-half inch silver button engraved with, "Button, Button, Who's Got The Button Tingue?" About 50,000 of these buttons and a couple of the original charm strings are currently in the Raymond E. Baldwin Museum Connecticut in Hartford; but are not on display, due to lack of space.

There was a widespread rumor that Queen Victoria offered prizes to any lass who made a string of 999 buttons. One woman described in a 1944 magazine when she was a young girl how she had responded to the rumor that the Queen would send enough Scottish plaid for a complete outfit to girls who collected the 999 buttons. The girl hunted buttons and kept them in a shoe box until she had the 999. Her father discouraged her from sending them to the queen because he suspected the offer was but a rumor. Disenchanted, she later married and gave the string to a button collector.

The charm string fad faded soon after the turn of the century. There were different kinds of button strings in the 1900s, sometimes strung to encourage young people in the hobby of button collecting. Experienced, modern-day button collectors liked to keep strings of duplicate buttons for trading purposes, just as the young ladies in the 1800s did for their charm strings.

In the 1930s during the Depression, another kind of button string evolved. These strings consisted of buttons of the same design usually strung together with a piece of cotton by a thrifty housewife who removed them before discarding an unwanted garment on which they had been sewn.

Although women were the usual button string owners, there are several documented instances where men have strung buttons on strings too. In fact, the longest button string on record was made by Charlie Miller, who reported in the 1960s that his string was over 100 feet long. Also in the 1960s, a woman in Lancaster, Pennsylvania, remembered that her father had a button string when she was a little girl. A man named Robert Hill also was known to have made one. Another was put together by a man, who as a carpenter had found a box of old buttons in a deserted house. He added to the string all the buttons he acquired over a twenty-year period.

Button strings have proved to be an informative guide to the variety of buttons manufactured and used in the 1800s. However, not many original button strings are intact. Most have been broken either intentionally, accidentally or by deterioration. Many button collectors got started by dismantling old button strings.

Button Buffs
(Button Collectors)

The young women who put buttons on charm strings in the Victorian Period were the first major group of button collectors. Before that there were only a few known individuals who collected buttons for reasons other than to wear them. One was Captain Luis Fenollosa Emilio, a man who fought in the Civil War. Collecting buttons became a life-time project for him, and he wrote a book, *The Emilio Collection of Military Buttons,* printed in 1911. His collection eventually went to the Essex Institute in Salem, Massachusetts.

There were also a few noteworthy button collectors in England and France in the 1800s. Lady Charlotte Schreiber is known for the large collection she left to the Victoria and Albert Museum in London. Lady Dorothy Nevill specialized in collecting thread buttons made by the cottagers of Dorset. The most famous early collection of buttons was assembled by Baroness Edmond de Rothschild and is now on display in the Rothchild family mansion owned by the British National Trust at Waddesdon Manor in Buckinghamshire, England. As early as 1860 in Brussels, Belgium, a collection of 18th century buttons was assembled and displayed on both sides of a screen in a castle.

Modern button collecting began in America as a hobby in the Depression after a woman named Gertrude Patterson talked about it enthusiastically in 1938 on the radio program "Hobby Lobby." Her comments created a sensation among American women; since they had more time than money, and buttons were plentiful and inexpensive. Button collecting quickly rose to one of the top three hobbies, along with stamp and coin collecting. By the mid-1900s, button collecting was the fastest growing hobby in the United States with an estimated 30,000 collectors. In an official proclamation in 1968, Minnesota's Governor Harold LeVander stated that button collecting was the third most popular hobby in the country. Hobby magazines as late as 1989 still ranked it third in popularity behind only stamps and coins.

Button collectors in the United States organized in 1939 to form the

Button Buffs

National Button Society, the oldest and largest in the world. Button clubs became very popular for American women. Club meetings were exuberantly started with "rouser songs," and holidays were elaborately celebrated with button-related club parties. Today there are over 4600 members in the National Button Society, representing fifteen countries, and the enrollment is increasing every year. There are also state and local chapters and independent clubs.

The National Button Society and the state chapters have annual conventions in the United States where buttons are displayed and sold. Members compete against each other with buttons which are arranged on trays according to material or subject matter. Collectors must follow very precise rules for these competitions. In producing trays, collectors act like curators

Award winning tray of "inanimate object" buttons by Lucille Weingarten

putting together museum shows. Judges then award prizes for the best trays, based on technical and aesthetic qualities.

The first and foremost rule for button competitors is, "Thou shalt not borrow buttons for competitive trays." Nor should a button be bought cheaply, then "sold" back to the original owner after the competition.

Button collectors walk from table to table at button shows carefully examining buttons, often with magnifiers to see the fine detail. They push their hands and fingers through "poke" boxes, bowls or trays of inexpensive buttons for sale. What might be considered odd behavior to the uneducated button person is actually a button detective at work. One might see a collector clinking a button against teeth, pricking it with a hot pin or holding a magnet next to it. She or he might also smell the button or plop it in a glass of water. These are all little tests to determine the button's material.

The buttons displayed at these conventions are truly splendorous. Button prices can vary from twenty-five cents for a "poke box button" to several thousand dollars for a rare button from the eighteenth century. The *Los Angeles Times* reported about the California State Button Show: "There wasn't a zipper in sight. Had there of been, it would probably have been carved, jeweled and signed."

The British Button Society was founded in 1976 and has about 350 members, plus regional chapters. The British Button Society has two annual meetings where buttons are displayed and sold, and informative talks are given.

Of course, there are innumerable button collectors who aren't members of any club. And there are club members who display their buttons on their clothes, wear them as jewelry or cover objects with them.

In the past, one of the best sources of buttons for button collectors was from paper mills that made fine rag paper. Before the rags could be chemically processed to produce the pulp that would become the 100 percent rag paper, workers removed all the buttons. The upper and middle class and wealthy families did not bother to save buttons.

However, most collectors have found their old buttons in grandmothers' or neighbors' buttons boxes, in attics and old trunks and on charm strings. A collector from New Hampshire wrote that the six sweetest phrases in our language are:

"I love you.
Dinner is served.
All is forgiven.
Sleep until noon.
Keep the change.
And would you like to look through Granny's old button box?"

Unfortunately, there aren't many of Granny's old button boxes left, but old buttons can still be bought at flea markets, rummage sales, garage sales, antique shops and antique shows, and in England at boot fairs and jumble sales. Nowadays, the most common sources for old buttons are button dealers, mail order businesses, video auctions and live auctions.

American button collectors have a long-standing reputation for fierce determination in getting their buttons. Sometimes acquiring an antique button requires the skill of a detective and the persuasion of a salesperson. In the 1940s, Mrs. R. H. Johnston was known as the "Button Lady." She tried repeatedly to persuade a woman to sell a George Washington inaugural button, but the woman wouldn't sell.

When Mrs. Johnston learned that the woman had wanted new kitchen linoleum for ten years, Mrs. Johnston traded her a new kitchen floor for the button!

Other collectors have found prize buttons digging in farm land and backyards, and on virtually any source of old clothes and sewing material. Collectors of Civil War memorabilia, using metal detectors to hunt for metal objects, have often turned up metal buttons.

California button dealer and collector Diane Ford once took her friend, Flora Weddington, who hadn't been to a button show for ten years, to a regional show. Flora floated through the day, happily dazed and spent all but $17 of her money. Diane took her to dinner that evening and insisted on paying for Flora's dinner. Flora said, "If I'd known that, I'd have spent $17 more on buttons!"

Millicent Safro and the late Diana Epstein are two of the most well-known button collectors. Ms. Safro owns the Tender Buttons store in New York City, named after Gertrude Stein's book, *Tender Buttons,* which is a tribute to insignificant objects such as button mushrooms. Tender Buttons is one of the most eclectic and comprehensive button stores in the world. Ms. Epstein and Ms. Safro have given button-themed parties at the store where they served marinated button mushrooms and played their favorite album—a recording of every rendition ever made of "Button Up Your Overcoat."

Another one-of-its-kind is the Button Museum in Ross-on-Wye in England. It opened in 1991, displaying about 10,000 buttons from the collection of Gillian and Alan Meredith. In 1992, it received the prestigious "Come to Britain Award," known as a tourism "Oscar" by the British Tourist Authority.

The button-collecting world has its share of people who are obsessive about their endeavor. In *Maine Charm String,* Elinor Graham wrote of one of her characters, "As far as buttons were concerned, she became completely predatory. In fact, when she took time to examine her motives, it gave her cause to worry about her immortal soul."

A past president of the Arizona Button Society is quoted as having said, "I think if there were a fire, I'd grab my buttons first, my dog second and my husband on the way out."

Another well-known collector admits to filching a button right off a flight attendant's uniform when it was hanging by the bathroom in an airplane. She carries a little pair of scissors with her, so her job was neat and tidy.

When asked how his mother got so many buttons, Frieda Warther's son, of the Warther Museum in Dover, Ohio, often replies, "She begged, borrowed, bought and in the end, she even stole." He explains that his mom taught Sunday School for years and was a good Christian woman. But when she was in her 90s, she found herself in a nursing home with a broken hip. One day a nurse came to work wearing a London Fog raincoat. When the nurse left for home that evening, there wasn't a button left on it!

When Dalton Stevens, known as the Button King, was a guest on the Late Night Show with David Letterman, he reportedly snipped a button off Lettermen's clothes. Mr. Stevens is known for covering almost everything in sight with buttons.

Another collector tells of nearly being thrown in jail in Mexico for adoringly touching an elaborate button on a Mexican police officer's uniform.

In his *Complete Book of Collecting Hobbies,* William Paul Bricker said about button collecting, "Either build an addition to the house or don't go into the button business. It's like raising rabbits."

Button collectors have long been accused of button thefts. In 1946, five hundred women became unmanageable at a store sale of nylon stockings. Police arrived to control the crowd. The only casualty was a policeman who lost the buttons from his uniform. A button collector was suspected.

When Colonel Frank Borman, the astronaut who circled the moon, visited Paris, he was greeted by French celebrities and huge crowds who clapped, cheered and begged for his autograph. When he left, two buttons were missing from his coat. It was thought he was victimized by a button collector.

In the 1940s, a newspaper article indicated that police were on the lookout for a button collector who snipped buttons off six garments in a store in Elkhart, Indiana.

When Edith Guetz from Arizona boarded a Royal Viking ship for a cruise, the first thing she did was inquire about getting a uniform button for her collection. That evening Edith was having dinner at the captain's table, and the lady at her side asked if she had swiped the missing button from the captain's jacket. Edith proclaimed her innocence, but said she wished it had been her. The captain ripped off the remaining button on his uniform and handed it to Edith. He said, "One button is no better than none." Edith was sure he meant in *that* situation.

Even though button collectors are accused, often humorously, of stealing buttons, the hobby is respectable and encouraged today. It wasn't always the case. In an 1887 issue of "The Northern Messenger," an article on the values of button collecting referred to it as "an objectionable fad . . . an obnoxious and slang-inspiring craze." This attitude changed, for as soon as 1896, the *Standard Designer* said, ". . . and we perhaps may hear of button collections becoming the rage, and why not? for they have arrived at that state of perfection that to call them works of art would not be exaggerating." In 1942, *Antiques Magazine* quoted the preceding quote saying, ". . . they probably had no idea that not fifty years afterward the buttons they described so lovingly . . . would be quite as enthusiastically collected as antiques . . ."

Button collectors' houses often reflect their hobby with displays of buttons, either mounted on trays on walls or grouped in jars or other decorative containers. Some collectors use button decor extensively. Freddie Speights has a "cupid nook" in his house to show off buttons featuring cupids. Formerly a linen closet, the nook has a large, bronze cupid with water fountains on each side, and the walls are lined with trays of cupid buttons. Another collector has a living room burlap-covered screen with 3500 buttons on it.

Family members of button collectors are often supportive and may even join the pursuit of finding buttons. However, sometimes family members, especially spouses, are bewildered if the collector seems addicted to the hobby or spends too much money on it. One woman says her family thought at first that her button collecting was a joke. After a year of collecting, the results were a bulging closet, boxes under the bed and a dining room table cluttered with buttons. Her family now thinks it's a nightmare!

In 1946, an article written by a button collector for a women's magazine said, "One of the consequences to being a button collector is that you may never again want to sew a button anywhere except on one of those big, beautiful exhibition cards." Or as a sign in the home of another collector says, "Buttons forever. Housework whenever."

When a reporter from the *Los Angeles Times* asked a button collector about the value of buttons at an annual button show, the woman hesitated. "You see," she said, "the girls don't want their husbands to know what they pay for some of their buttons." Another woman expressed it, "Our husbands have no idea how much we spend on buttons."

Collector Janet White in California received a handmade birthday card from her son that featured a "Common Button Imp" which he created along with the message, "Just a friendly warning . . . Every pursuit has its dangers."

Common *Button Imp.* This pesky creature is a bane to collectors. (Indigenous to North America).

(Courtesy of Roger White)

Eighty-two-year-old Rachel Leslie in Vermont started collecting buttons in 1935, and on each date asked her boyfriend to visit people with button boxes. She says he wasn't too excited about spending the evenings looking at buttons. He must not have minded too much though, since they've been married now for 55 years.

Faye Wolfe, daughter of a button collector, tells of her first job away from home at a Girls' Scout camp. Her mother made her late for her first day because she had to stop at every five and dime and dry goods store looking for buttons between Detroit, Michigan, and Morrow, Ohio. However, Faye became a button collector herself.

Like Faye, many button collectors get their start because a parent or other relative collected. Marge Spieldenner in California used to play with the buttons in her grandma's collection when she was little. When her grandma died, Marge was to inherit the collection. She went to her first button club meeting with the intention of selling the buttons. Instead she became a collector. Her daughter also became an avid collector before she discovered boys, and her son decorated his college dorm walls with trays of military buttons. Even Marge's granddaughter now plays with buttons.

Alice Banta from New York became a collector when she inherited a bathtub full of buttons from her husband's aunt.

Janel Marchi from California inherited a huge button collection from her great, great aunt because her grandmother didn't want them. In fact her grandmother, who was active politically in the women's suffrage movement, scoffed at the idea. Today Janel has added more than 4000 buttons to the collection and hopes her great, great aunt is smiling. She knows her grandmother must be, as Janel has a button collection *and* a career.

Jerry Fine, owner of the store, Antiquewear, in Marblehead, Massachusetts, got his inspiration for button collecting from the "True Love" button (see author's Introduction) among the beautiful and rare ones in his mother's extensive collection. Jerry decided to start his own collection when his mother told him that during the 1920s and 30s, women took buttons to jewelers to have them made into pins. He now specializes in making exquisite jewelry from antique buttons which feature written histories of the buttons.

Sometimes parents have caught the "button bug" from their children. Peggy Ann Osborne began collecting buttons when she was twenty-two years old. She became such a button fanatic that her mother, Mary Louise VandeBerg, told her that she was no fun anymore because all she could talk about were buttons. Peggy Ann went on to write numerous and acclaimed books about buttons. She also managed to convert Mary Louise who has become something of a fanatic herself, having won many awards in National Button Show competitions.

Button collecting is indeed contagious. Ida Mae Reeves in Arizona was sixty-seven years old and thought "people who chased buttons were crazy." Despite these initial thoughts, Ida "got hooked" and chased buttons herself until her death at ninety-seven.

Button collectors distinguish between accumulating buttons and collecting them. True button collectors, as a result of their hobby, are extremely-well educated people, who are usually delighted to share their knowledge. Early button collectors studied prehistoric remains, costumes, old fashion magazines and documents, manuscripts, diaries, letters, wills, inventories, bills, memorial brasses, graves, needlework books, effigies, tapestries and paintings to gain knowledge about buttons.

Serious button collectors today still like to know how, when and where buttons were made. They study buttons for the materials used, method of construction, decoration, manufacturer, history, backmarks, hallmarks and subject matter. Since buttons have encompassed nearly every conceivable subject, their study provides a broad liberal arts education, including obscure bits of fascinating information. For example, while studying buttons with dogs on them, it was learned that once the people of Ethiopia elected a dog king. A study of military buttons uncovered the story of "Old Abe," the only eagle to be inducted into the service of the United States Infantry. Turkey buttons taught collectors the strange history of turkeys; and that if Benjamin Franklin would have had his way, the turkey would have been our national bird.

In addition to uncovering history and adding enormously to mankind's wealth of knowledge, button collectors have been associated with charitable causes for more than 100 years. The button-covered costermongers (vegetable and fruit hawkers) in London, known as the Pearly Kings and Queens, are famous for their financial contributions to the hospitals in England starting in the late 1800s. At that time in England there was no National Health Service, so it was essential that people continually raise money for the hospitals to operate.

In the 1940s, members of the Acorn Button Club in Connecticut visited the famous Tingue button collection in the state capital, where it was being stored in an unlighted corner. The members used flashlights to examine the exquisite collection of over 90,000 buttons and found them in a state of deterioration. They obtained permission from the governor to restore them as a club project and spent two years doing so. The collection, which accurately represents the buttons worn by early American settlers, was then proudly displayed in the Museum of the Connecticut State Library for the appreciation of the public.

Charm string from Tingue Collection (Courtesy of Museum of Connecticut History)

It took Frieda Warther more than thirty-five years to assemble the buttons that cover the walls and ceiling of the Button House at the Warther Museum in Dover, Ohio. As a young girl, Frieda immigrated to the United States from Switzerland with her family. It was her job as the oldest of thirteen children to go door to door selling the vegetables grown in their garden or the baked goods that her mother made. She wanted to be dressed up for this task but couldn't afford jewelry. Instead, she strung her mother's buttons on thread to make necklaces and bracelets which she wore. When her customers saw her, they contributed buttons. This was the start of Frieda's lifetime of button collecting.

The most famous button in Frieda's collection is from the second inaugural gown of Mrs. Abraham Lincoln. When Mrs. Lincoln's relatives inherited the gown, they plucked one button from it for Frieda before donating it to the Smithsonian Institute.

Frieda mounted her buttons on boards of masonite, each in a geometric quilt-like design. Of the first 50,000 buttons, no two are alike. This collection of over 73,000 buttons on boards eventually covered the walls and ceilings of a building called the Button House, a part of the Warther Museum, and is there for the education and enjoyment of the general public. No admission is charged for the button section of the museum.

In 1978, button collectors from thirty states and Canada published a book called *Recipes and Buttons* as a fund-raising project. Each recipe was accompanied by one or two appropriate buttons. For example, a camel button was shown on the page with a recipe for pickling tainted camel meat. The recipe was transcribed from an old tomb, but had not been tested and was not in any way guaranteed!

From 1973 through the early 1990s, buttons were collected by the late Monica Jones and her Button Committee in Bristol for the Church of England's Children Society. The Button Committee organized the nationwide button appeal and then cleaned, sorted, carded and priced the buttons. Millions of buttons were given and sold, profiting 32,000 pounds sterling for charity. One of the promotions was called "Start a Button Collection" and consisted of packs of nine interesting buttons mailed with useful advise for beginning collectors.

In one of its issues, the magazine *"Just Buttons"* asked, "Why do folks collect buttons?" The answer was that collectors have been bitten by the button "bug," which is a germ that has produced a mild form of disease called button fever. They become immune to other activities. But they have the energy to prowl in out-of-the-way places and to ransack attics. They also have become immune to ordinary ailments and are able to leave a sick bed to attend an auction in the worst weather, fatal to any ordinary person. They work long hours without tiring and develop what is known as an iron constitution. Life insurance companies should consider them excellent risks!

Button Bigwigs
(Buttons and Famous People)

People from all parts of the world have had interesting experiences with buttons, but it has often been famous people who have made the world more button conscious.

Famous people who received attention because of buttons they wore go back to the 1200s when the kings and members of their courts wore excessive and magnificent buttons. This custom was typical of the rulers of most major countries through the 1700s. Even in the 1800s when beautiful buttons were worn by commoners as well, Queen Victoria achieved international attention because of the jet mourning buttons she wore for the rest of her life after the death of Prince Albert.

As far back as the 1500s, the most well known and respected artists made buttons. Benvenuto Cellini, known as the greatest goldsmith of all time, made buttons which he considered his finest works.

It was not uncommon through the 1700s for prominent artists to be commissioned to make buttons. For some, button making was a popular sideline. Between portraits, painters painted buttons, sometimes signing them. We know from French wills that painters like Jean Baptiste Isabey and Jean Honore Fragonard painted buttons. Iasabey said in his autobiography that he "kept the pot boiling by painting buttons." Famous potters and sculptors made ceramic buttons and famous silversmiths engraved silver buttons. Fine cabinetmakers carved wooden buttons.

There are buttons in the Louvre with designs copied from famous painters like Jean Louis Andre Theodore Gericault (1791–1824). One represents Le Chasseur à Cheval (The Light Cavalryman), a painting of 1812. Another represents Le Cuirassier Blessé (The Wounded Cuirassier), a painting of 1814.

In the 20th century, famous artists Salvador Dali, Jean Cocteau and Jean Schlumberger designed buttons for the renowned couturier, Elsa Schiaparelli, whose shocking buttons inspired the fashion industry in the 1930s. She commissioned extravagant and decorative buttons for her distinctive outfits. Buttons played an essential role in Schiaparelli's art. She used incredible things to make her buttons: feathers, animals, caricatures, paperweights, chains and locks. Not one looked like a typical button.

Peter the Great of Russia was said to have mastered fourteen crafts, and one was button making, according to *National Geographic*. Legend says he handcarved an array of gold-framed ivory buttons with military themes as decoration for his coats.

According to Esther Forbes in her book, *Paul Revere and the World He Lived In*, Paul Revere made buttons in the 1700s. "Captain Cochran (a Neighbor) . . . ordered tortoise-shell buttons; Deacon Thomas Hill . . . gold buttons," are words from Revere's ledger. In 1782, Revere also sent his cousins in France small presents of silver buttons which he had made.

Moses Austin, son of Stephen Austin for whom the capital of Texas was named, was a button maker in the 1700s in Virginia. This avocation preceded the younger Austin's fame when he undertook the enterprise of carrying out his father's dream, colonizing Texas.

The famous English industrialist, Mathew Boulton, actually began his career as a button maker.

Another famed English inventor, Henry Clay, made buttons from papier mâché. In 1772 he patented this process of sticking paper together with gum to make a substance as hard as wood.

President George Washington bought conch shells from a struggling peddler on a Philadelphia street and had a brown velvet coat made up especially for the buttons made from the conches. It is kept at Mount Vernon.

Fastening clothes wasn't the only use that George Washington made of buttons; he also had a set of false teeth made from them!

King George III was known as the "Birmingham Boy" in England because he amused himself by making buttons with a turning lathe. (Birmingham was the center of the British button industry.) In 1770 he was caricatured in *The Button Maker's Jest Book*.

In the early 1800s in Blue Hill, Maine, acclaimed folk artist, Parson Jonathan Fisher, augmented his menial salary of $200 a year plus fifteen cords of wood, by making and selling buttons to support his ten children. He and his children, filed, pierced and made the buttons from bones of slaughtered animals.

Post Office Department buttons were designed by Benjamin Franklin.

Carl Faberge, the famous jeweler, made buttons that are among the rarest, most beautiful and most costly ever produced. One set of six, described in *The Art of Carl Faberge* were engraved gold enameled in opalescent white and set in silver with rose diamonds.

Dame Lucie Rie, the world-renowned British potter, worked for Bimini Ltd making glass buttons when she first moved from Vienna to London. She later produced her own line of ceramic buttons in natural shapes and colors. The small, delicate woman tied weights to her feet so she wouldn't fall into her kiln while working alone.

Wolfgang Amadeus Mozart was enormously fascinated by buttons and gave serious consideration to the wearing of them, as evidenced in this passage from *Letters of Mozart and His Family*, ". . . I must have a coat like that, for it is one that will really do justice to certain buttons which I have long been hankering after. I saw them once, when I was choosing some for a suit. They were in Brandau's button factory in the Kohlmarkt, opposite the Milano. They are mother-of-pearl with a few stones round the edge and a fine yellow stone in the center . . ."

Napoleon loved buttons so much that he had them made especially for him and then had the die that made the buttons destroyed so they could not be duplicated. The ladies of the court always saved their rarest jeweled buttons to wear in front of him, hoping to win his favor.

In the 1700s, Ethan Allen had a famous sword which was decorated with a dog's head, a symbol he had adopted. In 1779, he put dog-head buttons on his military uniform to match his sword.

Ralph Waldo Emerson's buttons were cloth covered instead of bone because he liked things of soft texture. His buttons usually wore out before his coats, so he had them covered again.

Charles Dickens had a fascination for buttons which was displayed in his writing and in his life. He was said to have leased his residence at 48 Doughty Street from 1837–1839 because he was attracted to it by a Beadle (a parish officer who kept order) at each gate who wore uniforms with the Doughty Arms on their buttons.

Before Kaiser Wilheim of Germany left for Holland, he had several sets of drawers filled with buttons of every kind. He frequently changed the buttons on his uniforms so that he could display these treasures.

Adolf Hitler wore military buttons that matched his soldiers' brass buttons, except Hitler's were solid gold.

James Buchanan Brady, who was known as Diamond Jim Brady, was so enamored with diamond buttons that even his underwear buttons were made of diamonds.

In the early 1900s, magician Max Malini became famous for a trick involving buttons. He bit off the buttons from the clothes of strangers and replaced them before the victims could say, "Max Malini."

Corse Payton, an actor and impresario in 1905 at the height of his fame, wore buttons made of solid gold coins on his coats.

Doris Hill, screen star in the 1920s, introduced "funny face" buttons to Hollywood by wearing a "Funny Face Frock," a suit trimmed with buttons on the jacket and down the front of the skirt. The buttons were bright fabric buttons with women's faces painted on them.

In the 1940s, Ingrid Bergman, Edward G. Robinson and the Duchess of Windsor regularly bought buttons at Jack Partridge's, the only button store in New York at the time.

During the same time span, actress Michele Morgan, had a coat made with ten buttons, each of which had her own fingerprint stamped on the center.

Jack Paar, the famous talk show host, overcame a speech impediment quickly by practicing his speech with buttons in his mouth. The buttons he used were from his mother's button box in their basement. This therapy worked because at age sixteen he became one of the youngest radio announcers in the United States.

A set of ruby-studded buttons that once belonged to Clark Gable was auctioned in Geneva and changed hands for $25,000.

Princess Grace of Monaco collected engraved and filigreed buttons to replace plain ones on her cashmere cardigans.

In the 1960s, an enterprise called The Old Buttons Shop in New Orleans sold buttons to the White House when the Kennedys occupied it. Jacqueline Kennedy collected French enamel buttons. Peter Lawford was a client too. His favorite buttons were reported to have been big filigreed silver buttons that attached to a vest and a button from the 1600s depicting a bullfighter.

Celebrities have bought their buttons for decades at the Tender Buttons shop in New York City. They have included Greta Garbo, Jane Powell, Calvin Klein, Mel Brooks, Burt Bacharach, Oleg Cassini, Bill Blass, Ralph Lauren, Bill Cosby, Susan Sarandon, Harry Belafonte, Ali McGraw, Mario Buatta, Brooke Shields, Candice Bergen, Julie Christie, Claudette Colbert, Catherine Deneuve, Rose Kennedy, Paloma Picasso, Sidney Poitier, Isabella Rossellini, Carly Simon, William Styron and Tom Wolfe. Kermit the Frog's Humphrey Bogart trench coat sported buttons especially designed and made by the store's owners, Millicent Safro and the late Diana Epstein.

The Button Store in Los Angles provides buttons for many of Hollywood's blockbuster movie and television costumes. For the movie "Hard Rain," five gross of costume buttons had to be re-dyed four times because they were constantly in chemically treated water.

Buyers for movie stars such as Bette Midler and Julia Roberts frequent The Button Store, often purchasing several sets of buttons for the same outfit so that the celebrity can choose the winning set of buttons to be used on the outfit. Actress Demi Moore likes buttons so much that she often keeps all the sets.

Brooke Shields got hooked on buttons when she was three. She had gone to a Third Avenue thrift shop in New York with her mother, and the woman who worked there gave her boxes of buttons to entertain her. Now she collects buttons and uses them for decoration purposes. She once repaired the damaged patio of her home in New Jersey by removing the border row of tiles and filling in the space with pearl buttons she had collected.

Another famous button collector and user was the French General and statesman, Charles de Gaulle. He specialized in collecting buttons from French military uniforms.

Even Barbie has been fascinated with buttons. To celebrate her thirtieth birthday in 1989, top designers created a luxurious new wardrobe for the doll. One of the creations was a black velvet dress with multicolored buttons.

As New York interior designer, Mario Buatto flew to Malcolm Forbes' 1989 birthday bash in Moroco, Buatto did what his tailor didn't have time to do. He sewed antique buttons on his new Ralph Lauren blazer.

"Buttons give off auras of good taste, art, wealth and magnificence," said author, Tom Wolfe, who wrote *Bonfire of the Vanities*. He uses an array of buttons to distinguish his white suits from one another, reported *The Wall Street Journal* in 1992.

Both Mario Buatta and Alexandra Stoddard use buttons to enliven decorating projects and accessorize homes. Ms. Stoddard uses them to give distinctive touches to pillows and upholstery.

Entertainers have frequently paid special attention to the buttons they wear while performing:

Colleen Moore wore a spectacular button-covered dancing costume in the silent film "Twinkletoes" in 1926.

In the 1929 movie, "The Cocoanuts," Harpo Marx ate the buttons off a bellman's vest. The buttons were made of licorice.

Once Danny Kaye sang "Buttons and Bows" at the London Pallidum wearing the "pearl button uniform" of England's famed Pearly King costume.

Danny Kaye

When Charles Laughton was cast to play the role of Captain Bligh in "Mutiny on the Bounty" in the 1950s, he went to the Old Bond Street firm of Gieves, who had made Bligh's uniforms. Laughton was able to get exact detailed descriptions of Bligh's uniforms, including the number of buttons, how they were spaced and which buttons worked and which were merely for display. Laughton ordered a duplicate wardrobe, right down to the last buttonhole.

In 1954, the producers of the Metro Goldwyn Meyer film, "Battle of the Nile," asked the editor of *British Buttons* to obtain exact replicas of the buttons worn by Admiral Nelson at Aboukir Bay in 1798. The editor traced the buttons to Edward Armfield & Co. Ltd in Birmingham. The firm's director found the correct design and tools and cleaned them up to produce the buttons which he sent to MGM with his compliments.

Liberace's elaborate costumes sparkled with diamond buttons. His costume caretaker was always greatly concerned about these diamond buttons, which cost $1,000 apiece when purchased in the 1960s.

In the 1970s musical, "Lorelei," Carol Channing wore twelve dazzling costumes that cost $65,000. The most remarkable costume was a wedding dress that was decorated with 2,000 buttons.

Liberace

The buttons on Barbra Streisand's coat in one of the costume-period scenes of the film, "On a Clear Day You Can See Forever," cost $1,000 per button. There were six Austrian, 14-karat, double-eagle, gold buttons, formerly belonging to Emperor Franz Josef. "It probably marks the first time in Hollywood history that a producer has spent buttons like money," Yves Montand said to producer Howard Koch.

Famous singers have their button stories, too. Mattiwilda Dobbs, soprano of the Metropolitan Opera Company in the 1960s, wore a special button whenever she sang the role of the Page in "The Masked Ball." The opera's plot was based upon the murder of King Gustavus III of Sweden, which took place at a midnight masquerade in the Stockholm Opera House in 1792. The button that Miss Dobbs wore was originally worn by King Gustavus on his court dress. It was reported that Miss Dobbs liked to fancy that he wore it on the night of the historic ball.

Dame Vera Llynn, the British Forces' Sweetheart who toured war zones singing, was never a star at school and was happy to leave at the age of fourteen. She took a job sewing on buttons at a button factory but lasted only one day before she quit. Her mother and father let her quit because she was earning more in a week singing than she could earn in a month from sewing buttons.

Joan Rivers, the entertainer and comedienne, also worked at one time for a button company. She was on the editorial staff of the B. Blumenthal Company (later became Blumenthal-Lansing), which manufactures LaMode buttons, among others.

Shirley Temple once sent a letter to a Patsy Ford as a token of appreciation for stamps sent by Ms. Ford. Attached to the letter was a button from the dress of one of Miss Temple's dresses worn in the movie, "Just Around the Corner."

Nuts and Bolts of Buttons
(Materials, Subjects and Techniques)

Buttons have been made of every possible existing material, have encompassed every conceivable subject and have employed every technique known in the fine arts, as well as the more crude, manual methods.

Most people are aware of buttons made from plastic, wood, metal, glass, fabric, pearl, shell, enamel, ceramic, clay and rhinestones. Fewer people know that buttons have been made of auto lubricant, paper, weeds, nuts, seeds, leaves, flowers, tree bark, pine cones, moss, milkweed pods, shell, seaweed, gutta percha (dried juice of an evergreen tree), linoleum, nylon, jet, rocks, cork, semiprecious and precious jewels, photographs, sealing wax, paraffin, beeswax, sulfide, polymer clay, metal foil, sequins, paper clips, safety pins, shoelaces, fish hooks, bobbins, padlocks, mahjongg pieces, European Loo chips (from the game Loo), poker chips, dice, microprocessors, circuit boards, holograms, biscuit dough and radioactive soil from Hiroshima.

Button materials that stretch the imagination have included fruits, vegetables, other unlikely foods and all kinds of animal parts, including those of humans.

Factories in both Germany and the United States put buttons made from blood on the market in the early 1900s. However, patent office records show that the idea of using blood to make buttons was tried in the United States earlier. In 1879, a patent was obtained for the manufacture of buttons made from blood, and in 1880 a second patent was granted for the mixture of powdered blood. The first method used whole blood and relied upon heat and pressure to produce coagulation. The second used powdered blood with gelatin or some other adhesive. Blood buttons were dark in color and expensive to make but compared well in appearance with the best buttons on the market. They weren't as durable as other buttons, however.

Both human and animal skins have been used to make buttons. The skin of young animals, sometimes obtained before birth from fetuses, was cut into small discs, painted and made into glass covered buttons.

Millicent Safro, owner of Tender Buttons in New York City, has buttons made from hippopotamus and giraffe skins.

In 1946, the magazine, *Just Buttons,* stated that the president of Waterbury Companies was seen wearing a button made of human skin which had been tanned and mounted in a gold-plated rim.

Hair of both humans and animals have been used for buttons. Throughout most of the 1800s, fashionable glass-covered buttons were made from braided hair. In the mid 1800s, another type of hair button that fastened ladies' dresses also became popular. These buttons were made of small beads formed of hair, clustered around a center of diamonds and mounted in gold.

Memorial buttons to honor the deceased were commonly made out of hair. These were meticulously braided or woven. Some buttons were hair painted. These buttons didn't use paint at all but relied entirely upon different colors and lengths to form intricate pictures.

Buttons were also embroidered with hair with stitches so fine that it seems human hands couldn't have accomplished such feats.

Horse and camel hairs have long been used for upholstery buttons because they make an extremely durable haircloth.

Mohair buttons from various animals have provided buttons that matched fabrics to create elegant looks.

Snake skin, rabbit fur, monkey fur, porcupine quills and leather have all been known to compose buttons. Handmade buttons from leather shoelaces tied into a series of knots were popular at one time. Even old leather shoes used to be recycled into buttons by treating them with chloride of sulfur, drying, grinding to a powder, mixing with glue or gum and pressing into button molds.

A man in New Orleans made and marketed buttons from the scales of giant gar fish. He carved the scales into the shape desired with a motor grinder and then used a power spray to color the scales, giving the buttons a pearly luster.

Animals have contributed teeth, hoofs, horns, claws, feathers, quills and bones for centuries to enable people to make buttons.

In the 1860s, English sportsmen wore waistcoats embroidered with foxes' heads and fastened with buttons sporting foxes' teeth.

In 1935, Field-Marshall Herman Goering went to a hunt dinner wearing silver-mounted buttons made from the teeth of elk that he had shot.

A tiger's toenail mounted in a silver button was once worn on a hunting coat in Japan.

Walrus' teeth, sharks' teeth and horses' teeth buttons, although considered grotesque nowadays, used to be set in brass or silver and proudly worn.

Even human teeth, especially gold-filled and those from babies, have found their way into buttons, sometimes encased in plastic, but not always.

There is mention of a cuff button made of the finest specimen of a human molar in the movie, "The Great Gatsby."

Animal horns and bones have been used for buttons, both in powdered form with other fibrous materials, or cut with holes drilled through them.

Bone historically has been first on the animal, then in the soup, then chewed on by the dog and finally made into highly polished buttons.

"Sourdough" buttons of California gold rush 49'ers were adopted from native Indians. The buttons were made from deer horn, with crude holes for sewing.

Beautifully carved and painted ivory buttons were abundant until ivory became scarce. The Chinese have made five-eighth-inch buttons of ivory with minute Chinese writing on them which are the texts of poems. On one such button the text reads: "In a mountain village with nothing to do; Quietly a day passes like a year." Vegetable ivory, made from the nuts of the tagua palm in South America now often substitute for ivory buttons.

Fish bones and fossils have also found their ways into buttons at one time or another.

Buttons made out of insects such as beetles, ants and butterflies didn't seem to "bug" our ancestors a bit, as the buttons have existed since the 1700s. A contemporary button collector has one from that century hanging on her wall. The beetle's corpse is perfectly preserved in its tiny tomb. The tomb is a two-inch disc enveloped in glass. After insects die, they dry up in the same shape, size and color. The exoskeletons that are left last indefinitely, but they are fragile. Therefore, buttons made from them are usually in protective glass or embedded in clear plastic or wax. Sometimes, just parts of the insects' bodies, such as butterfly wings, were used.

A couple in New York who own an exterminating company have a collection of more than 600 insect buttons.

Many foods have been used to make buttons. Seeds from persimmons and other fruits have been drilled with two holes and sewn on clothes. Peach, apricot and plum stones and olive pits have been carved into buttons. Dried peas and pieces of gourd have been covered with fabric to form buttons. Buttons have been made of gelatin that has been chemically treated and combined with glue.

In the early 1900s, there were plastic buttons that had seeds, grains, pasta and other edible tidbits encased in them. In the 1950s, Paris designers used buttons that had been made by first covering them with glue, then sprinkling wheat, corn, peas, sunflower seeds and rice over them. The designer Christian Dior created a line of buttons that looked as if they had been taken from a museum of primitive art. The button work with these materials was reminiscent of the 1800s when buttons had grains and corn stamped on them for designs and also featured buttons with seeds under glass.

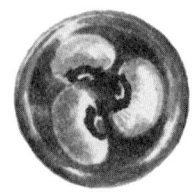

Thousands of people have buttoned their clothes with potatoes. Buttons made from potatoes are every bit as good looking as buttons of bone or ivory. When potatoes are treated with certain acids, they become almost as hard as stone, but they melt when a hot iron hits them.

In 1850, a patented formula for the filler in composition buttons used molasses and wheat flour. In 1888, there was a patent obtained to make buttons out of molasses, along with other fibrous materials and glycerin.

Chemical compounds used for making plastic buttons have consisted of all kinds of unlikely food products such as corncobs, bran, milk, beer and substances which might make a person blush.

A protein substance from milk called casein is used in the manufacture of synthetic pearl buttons and other plastic buttons. In the 1940s, it was learned that the vitamin riboflavin in milk caused the buttons to discolor. The vitamin was removed by a process developed at the University of Wisconsin by treating the casein with either warm alcohol or acetone.

The result was improved clear white buttons.

Milk is only one of the five materials that cows provide for our buttons. The others are horn, leather, bone and blood.

Every metal that exists has been made into buttons, and many metal buttons have been the result of recycling. In the 1700s and 1800s, melting down brass kettles when they sprung holes and making buttons from them was a common occurrence. One smart American button maker grabbed the market after the War of 1812 by getting all the brass utensils he could find and turning them into buttons. Another collected copper from old stills, sugar boilers and kettles for the same purpose. Pewter buttons were made from old plates, mugs and dishes.

Buttons were made from the residue of ammunition from World War I. These buttons sizzled and melted, emitting a pungent odor when they got close to open flames, however.

Buttons have been made from the sides of used tomato and other fruit cans, as well as from used shotgun shells and iron chains from prisons.

Another kind of metal recycling for buttons entails the use of coins. Coins, especially silver ones, were adapted for button use as early as the 1600s. Many are from Austria, Hungary, Spain and Mexico. In South

America, gouchos wear shanked coins as trim on their jackets and trousers.

After the French Revolution, low-value coins were used as buttons on French uniforms because they were cheaper than other buttons.

Coin buttons never seem to go completely out of style in the United States. They've been worn since Colonial craftsmen made button molds from gold coins, and jewelers converted silver coins into buttons. Buttons were often made of Spanish dollars in Colonial times. American Indians were also fond of coin buttons.

Coin buttons were especially fashionable in the last half of the 1800s. A wealthy man in Los Angeles, California, was known for wearing buttons made of gold dollars on the pocket flaps of a yellow satin waistcoat.

Buttons made from gold nuggets as large as one-half inch resulted from the Klondike Gold Rush in the late 1800s.

In the 1930s, buttons were made of sales tax tokens, which were valued in fractions of a cent. The most common were tokens from Arizona. They were made of copper with beautiful cacti designs and borders on them. It became so difficult to keep an adequate supply in circulation that aluminum was substituted for the copper.

In the 1960s, the European custom of converting coins into buttons was revived by button manufacturers in the United States. Shanks were soldered on small value coins from many different countries, and there was a steady demand for them. Imitation coin buttons became popular in the 1960s, although it was not a new concept. Old Roman and Greek coins were imitated in metal buttons in 1896. Buttons made in the 1960s, called "Forbidden Money," were perhaps the most well known because their manufacture was forbidden. Most of them imitated United States gold coins.

Another metal use of unusual interest for buttons pertains to the dipping of brass or copper buttons into gold. The Golden Age of Buttons from 1830–1880 was a time of splendorous buttons in England. Gilt buttons came in double gilt, treble gilt, fine gilt, best gilt and warranted rich gilt. Thirty thousand buttons, one inch in diameter, could be gilded with one ounce of gold, with 14,000 or 15,000 the number over which this quantity was commonly spread.

The commercial buttons made in the United States at the time of the American Revolution were delicate gilt buttons also. However, the Americans put so much gilt on them that many companies failed in this business. Scovill Manufacturing Company finally hired an Englishman to help them improve their product. He was sent to Birmingham to learn how to cast and roll brass and how to properly gild it. He also purchased equipment and brought a toolmaker to the United States.

There are other interesting uses of metal for button making. One is tole-painting on tin buttons. Another is a foil method where a thin leaf of copper, gold, silver or platinum is placed under a precious stone to make it look transparent or to deepen the color. Reflector buttons use metal backs and glass with a layer of paint or colored foil in between. Still another usage is of niccolite, the shiny underneath metal in buttons that twinkle. One studio button maker (makes hand-crafted buttons especially for collectors) has specialized in handmade, tiny replicas of the tin cookie cutters that our grandmothers used.

Wood buttons became very popular during World War I, due to metal shortages. Hundreds of varieties of trees have provided buttons, some being starkly simple while others such as wood mosaics are so intricate that they have hundreds of pieces. Some have used as many as five kinds of wood in one button. The simplest of these mosaics are two-color checkerboard designs.

The simplest wooden buttons are made from scraps, some of which have come from driftwood and cigar boxes.

Some button makers have specialized in making wooden buttons from historic buildings before they have collapsed or been destroyed.

Paper, a product of cotton, hemp or wood, has also been used in several ways to make buttons. Miniature portraits painted on paper and covered with glass go back several centuries. In 1846, an English button maker and inventor patented paper for buttons that imitated silk and other fabric. The paper was as supple as cloth and as smoothly stretched. It was used as a background for pen and ink drawings combined with brush work in black. Then the surface was heavily varnished.

Paper has been used for making shoe buttons, lithographed buttons, and as a backing for parts of metal buttons. For papier mâché buttons, paper pulp is combined with glue and other ingredients.

Cut paper has also produced elaborately complicated designs on buttons. Simple paper buttons have come from cardboard and plain paper pulp.

In the 1700s, paper dolls under protective glass were featured on buttons. The dolls wore fabric clothes but had paper legs, arms and heads that moved freely about.

Most people are familiar with fabric-covered buttons. There have been velvet perfume buttons and elaborate passamenterie buttons on silk with metallic threads, sequins and beads of the 1700s. Button makers in France

Nuts and Bolts of Buttons

had to serve a nine-year apprenticeship before they could officially make these passamenterie buttons.

In the 1800s, fabric covered buttons that were actually dried peas covered with leftover fabric from the making of the dresses were worn on the simplest wash dresses.

Prior to the 1880s, however, most fabric buttons were made in factories. When button styles were such that they matched the garment fabric, small hand machines with metal molds appeared in department stores, and clerks covered the buttons right there.

Fabrics have also been used to produce lace, tapestry, embroidered, crocheted, knitted, and painted buttons.

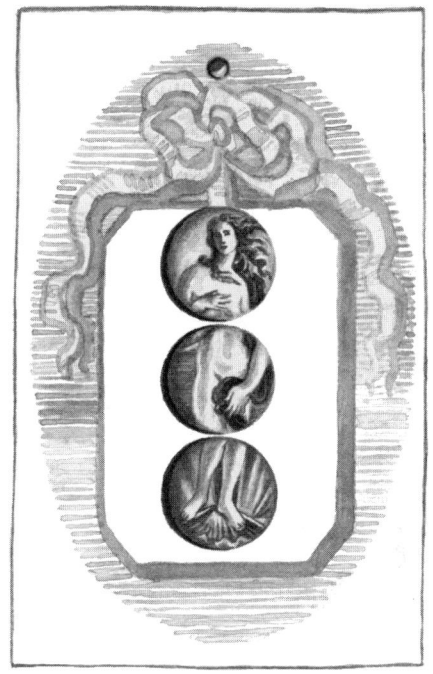

Buttons were made of hard rubber after Charles Goodyear invented vulcanized rubber in 1839 by accidentally dropping a mixture of rubber and sulfur on a hot stove. In 1851, Goodyear patented the process for button making, and he made buttons decorated with birds, dragons and classical heads. These buttons were popular in the United States; but due to a peculiar odor that emanated from them, they were never received well in Europe.

Buttons using combinations of materials have existed from a very early time, and every material probably at one time or other has been used with every other material. Some buttons have used as many as six different materials. These combinations have produced some of the most breathtakingly beautiful works of art in the button kingdom. Some of these material marriages seem most surprising, however, such as ball-shaped glass buttons that have cotton filling!

Subjects for buttons have come from nature and from life itself. Nearly every living thing, as well as inanimate thing, that exists has been displayed on a button. Even some that haven't existed are on buttons, like the sphinx, Pegasus, winged lion, mermaid, unicorn and dragon.

Prehistoric buttons from the earliest period had geometrical designs carved on them. Later periods from 2000 BCE were of the picture type, showing animals, birds and trees.

Through the 1800s, button makers were greatly influenced in their design of buttons by the events of the time—much more so than button makers today. Nothing of consequence happened that wasn't recorded on a button—inaugurations, coronations, wars, art, sports and religious events, political and historical happenings. Scenes appeared on buttons from theatrical productions, operas, novels, poems, fairy tales, famous and infamous people and places and etchings from books and magazines. Shakespeare's work is well represented in button form.

Popular singers and actors were depicted on several different styles of buttons. Dozens of Kate Greenaway's illustrations have found their ways onto buttons. Children's buttons from the 1800s were taken from famous stories by the Brothers' Grimm and Aesop. Exquisitely made scenes from operas have appeared on buttons.

Numerous scenes from mythology and the Bible, as well as erotica, have appeared on buttons. In the latter part of the 1800s, there was an amusing group of lithographed waistcoat buttons showing "vices." They were called the "Road to Ruin" or "Downfall of Man" buttons and showed symbols of wine, women, song, racing and gambling. These scandalous buttons weren't considered proper to be worn in the presence of decent women, so men wore them at their clubs.

In the 1920–1940s, buttons were made of most of the comic characters. Blondie and Dagwood Bumstead, Little Henry, Dick Tracy, Winnie

Winkle, Popeye, Olive Oyl, Bruno and every Disney character of the time all found their way onto buttons.

Button makers have never been without a sense of amusement in their designs. The early rebus buttons with their word puzzles and riddles often brought smiles to people's faces. Later, political campaign buttons frequently brought belly laughs. At one time buttons featuring replicas of the human eye, complete with lashes and eyebrows, were in vogue and are still made today. Insects were encased in glass on buttons in such a way that they appeared to move, as though alive. Hooks, eyes and zippers, all competitors, have been displayed on buttons. A woman in England has a button from a man's trouser fly, inscribed "Gentlemen Only."

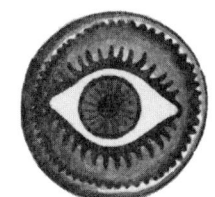

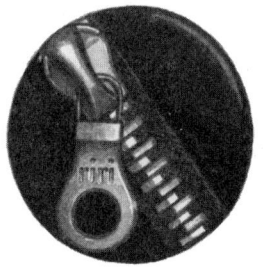

The darker sides of life are also well-represented on buttons. Graphic scenes from wars, executions and hunting expeditions used to be popular subjects for buttons. The gruesome death's head buttons, which are human-skull shaped, began to be worn in the 1500s. In 1583, Henry III had eighteen dozen large silver buttons made in this shape to be worn on his clothes. The design has been used all through the centuries, including the 20th century.

In earlier times most professions, businesses and organizations had their own button designs. Even bull breeders in Spain had their own insignias in button form, and it was quite common for ranchers to have their brands on the leather or metal buttons they wore.

Some of the more intriguing subjects on buttons in porcelain are the ones copying the designs and sometimes the actual miniature pieces of china made by Royal Doulton, Serves, Copenhagen, Chantilly, Lamoges, Minton, Meissen and Wedgwood.

Techniques for button making go far beyond the commonly noticed ones of painting, enameling, needle working, woodworking, metallurgy and plastic molding. Buttons have also been products of sandblasting, carving, piercing, stenciling, spattering, sculpture, gilding, drawing, inlaying, japaning, engraving, etching, casting, and glass blowing. The arts of damascene, tole, tintype, scrimshaw, filigree, pyrography, intaglio, lithography, Chinese scratch carving and internal carving have all been employed to produce buttons.

Tromp L'oeil was an unusual art used for buttons in the late 1700s. It literally means fooling the eye. The accurate representation of details on the buttons created an illusion of reality. The depth and form gave, for instance, a deck of cards painted on ivory under glass, an illusionary appearance of actual cards.

Silver point drawing used a pen holder with a point of pure sharpened silver. This was used to draw on buttons before pencils were invented.

Paperweight buttons have been made that are perfect miniature copies of Baccarat paperweights from the 1800s.

By the end of the 1800s, plastic buttons began to replace most of the other materials. Plastic buttons were light, colorful and cheap, and by the end of the 1920s had become the predominate material out of which buttons were made.

There has been a world-wide emergence in interest and usage of novel fashion buttons which began with designer Patrick Kelly's button-laden fashion collection in 1985 and continues today.

Modern buttons still commemorate major news and historic events. Some of the more significant ones in the twentieth century have represented the coronations of Queen Elizabeth, Prince Ahito and Princess Michiko and Gustav VI, the scandal of the "$64,000 Question" television show, the completion of Mt. Rushmore and the launching of Sputnik. Perhaps the most amazing was the button made in 1964 with Abraham Lincoln's Gettysburg Address engraved on it to commemorate the American Civil War.

However, most buttons nowadays sadly aren't nearly as beautiful, as unique or as well-made as antique buttons, although a few designers and studio button makers have continued to treat button making as an art. Buttons today that more often reflect current events are in plastic pin-back form, and these aren't really buttons at all.

Uniform Buttons That Went to War
(And Ones That Stayed Home)

Uniform buttons range from the obvious, such as military and transportation buttons, to the more obscure such as those of businesses, private clubs and department stores. Even bridle buttons for horses have sometimes been uniform buttons, as on the horses of the Mounted Police of Philadelphia.

Buttons on military uniforms have always been objects of great pride to the men and women who wore them. Nearly all countries use military buttons as marks of honor. Between 1762 and 1914, France alone had 370 military buttons. The British Army during World War I used 367 different buttons on their uniforms. Their buttons were considered so important to front-line troops that any kind of button could be requisitioned and delivered within eight hours. The British Army reportedly spent $500,000 per year just for the paste used to polish brass buttons.

Military buttons were so revered during World War II that American families sent to their loved ones overseas button shining kits called "Your Buddy Button Shiner." Inside was a polishing cloth, and on the back of the box was an address label.

Buttons have been so important to military services that traditionally when a soldier was dishonorably discharged, his buttons were stripped from his uniform in public because he was deemed unworthy to wear the emblem of his country.

Danny Deever got more than a discharge after his buttons were taken in Rudyard Kipling's famous poem:

"For they're hangin' Danny Deever,
you can 'hear the Dead March play,
The regiment's in 'ollow square—they're hangin' him today;
They've taken of his buttons off and cut his stripes away,
An' they're hangin' Danny Deever in the mornin'."

The question, "Could a soldier be a soldier without his brass buttons?" was raised when the United States entered World War II. The answer was, "No." Officials in Washington, D. C. realized that in modern warfare, uniforms should be dull in color to give a soldier low visibility to the enemy. Few things reflected sunlight as brightly as brass buttons. But no one would take the responsibility for the brass buttons' abolition. The buttons were given a dull coating which soon wore off.

The British evidently put good sense over sentimentality in the late 1700s when the first rifles were put into military use and camouflage became an important issue. They implemented the use of black buttons for the uniforms on the King's Royal Rifle Corps instead of brass, silver or gilt buttons.

In the Civil War, black Goodyear rubber buttons were worn on the uniforms of the North's Berdan's Sharpshooters because they found, like the British, that the black buttons didn't glisten in the sun.

The Navy men weren't so agreeable about giving up the traditional buttons on their uniforms in 1948. They refused to wear the new zipper sailor suit. They took the suits to tailors and had the zipper removed, or they ordered the old-fashioned suits with the thirteen buttons. Admiral Arleigh Burke, Chief of Naval Operations, admitted defeat in the "Battle of the Buttons." He said, "There is no use issuing orders men will not obey," as he issued orders restoring the old buttoned suits.

Prior to official orders around 1750, fighting forces in England and France were free to dress as they wished. They wore the same kinds of buttons as civilians and chose any pattern they wanted. Around 1760, both countries authorized the placement of numbers and emblems on their military buttons. The Royal Warrant of 1768 for the British Army stated that buttons on the uniforms would reflect the regiment and the initial letter of the title of the corps.

Until the early 1800s, U. S. military officers were permitted wide latitude in selecting their personal uniforms and buttons. Soldiers had official buttons for their uniforms in the War of 1812. In 1821, strict uniform regulations were introduced. The buttons became more functional and less artistic.

After 1830, U. S. Army officers weren't allowed to wear citizen's clothes when in camps or garrisons or marches. However, until 1863, they could still wear military clothes for civilian affairs. They had to wear plain dark blue coats, with the buttons designating their respective corps, regiments or departments, and the coats could not be worn for military use. This privilege was withdrawn in 1872, after which officers not on duty could wear a buff, white or blue vest with small prescribed buttons.

"Half-pay" buttons were worn by U. S. officers who were retired on half pay during the peace period following the Revolutionary and Napoleonic Wars, lasting from 1815 to around 1860. In the mid-1800s, approximately 80% of the officers were on half pay.

Button shortages have sometimes presented problems. Such was the case when the Scoville Manufacturing Company in Connecticut supplied the U. S. Army with a huge order of buttons for the War of 1812. However, the Army couldn't get enough cloth to make all the uniforms and attempted to return half the buttons to the Scoville Company. No buttons were returned from the Army because Scoville sent a representative to John Astor's sheep ranch to buy wool to provide the uniforms the Army needed. The representative sent a sample of the wool to the Scoville factory with a note that said, "Please write me a very discouraging note about the sample I am sending you and leave the rest to me." The sheep were sheared on Scoville terms a few days later, and Scoville set up a textile mill that provided military uniforms for nearly ten years.

Buttons were made commercially for the first time in the U. S. around 1750. The output of brass and pewter buttons was so small, however, that when the American Revolution broke out in 1775, most of the uniform buttons for American soldiers were imported from France. Some pewter buttons were made by the soldiers themselves using molds, as confirmed by archaeologists in the 1900s.

When the U. S. faced button shortages during both the Revolutionary and 1812 Wars because of the nonimportation policy, brass buttons were made from melted-down brass pots, pans and kettles. Pewter buttons were made from melted-down plates, mugs and dishes bought throughout the land. The button molds were bought from Yankee peddlers, who traveled from town to town.

During the Civil War in 1861–1865, buttons in the South were desperately scarce. At the outbreak of the war, there wasn't a single button factory in

Civil War acorn button

the South. Soldiers of the Northern armies and sailors in the navy needed buttons, too, but they were easy to get because there were many button factories in the North. The shipping of manufactured goods was embargoed, and the South's transportation system fell into disrepair. Blockade runners were often caught with small arms, ammunition and buttons.

Officers and wealthier Southerners could get some buttons imported from Europe, but the North often blockaded the ships. In fact, there were large shipments of Confederate buttons that never left the factories in England. Confederate soldiers had to rely on archaic methods of crudely-made buttons, some of which were homemade, to supply their demand. Some buttons were made, using improvised tools and scrap metal, by local people who had never before made buttons. Civilian buttons of brass, wood, bone, horn and glass were used in emergencies. Some even wore acorns as buttons.

It is also well documented that buttons from dead or captured Union soldiers were used by the Southern soldiers. If there was no need for buttons in the immediate area, the Union buttons would be melted down and used for making a variety of other military items.

In the years following the Civil War, numerous changeable and reversible buttons were invented and patented. These buttons, which were also popular with train conductors, police and firemen, conveniently converted a veteran's civilian coat into an official uniform and vice-versa.

Not all military uniform buttons have stayed on the uniforms of soldiers. During the American Revolution, soldier Jeremiah Greenman was captured by the British and imprisoned in Quebec. He wrote in his diary that there was no recreation for the prisoners, so they removed metal buttons from their garments and made a fife with them and played music to "keep up their hearts."

Other uniform buttons saved their wearers' lives in the Battle of Carrickfergus in Ireland in 1778. When the 62nd Regiment of Foot ran out of ammunition, they tore off their buttons and fired them to maintain their defense.

Regimental gold buttons provide the clasps on a large book in the Library of Congress. The book was acquired from the Winter Palace Library of the last Czar of Russia and tells the history of the Czar's own regiment. The book has binding made of the actual uniform of the soldiers.

Some Civil War uniform buttons were adapted into hooks to fasten knit shawls. These were invented by an army surgeon for fastening soldiers' blankets and for tent hooks.

Major Abner R. Small told of another button that didn't stay on a uniform in his memoirs of Civil War camp and prisoner life in *The Road to Richmond*. During the war, soup was made from a compound that came in dried, partable sheets. On one occasion, a button evidently fell into and floated on top of this government-rationed soup. Major Small wrote, "Ben once brought in just before dinner a piece with a big horn button in it, and wanted to know 'if dat 'ere was celery or cabbage?'"

Copperhead was a name given in the 1860s to members of the Democratic party in the northern states who opposed the Civil War. The name originated from the buttons worn by the opponents of the war. The buttons were the heads of Liberty that had been cut out of copper cents.

After the Civil War, an order was issued forbidding the wearing of Confederate uniforms. But the order had to be modified to ban only the Confederate buttons or insignia of rank, because few of the former Confederate soldiers had any clothing except their uniforms. There were problems with this order also, since there were no other buttons to replace the military ones, and buttons were necessary to keep the pants on and the coats buttoned. Buttons had to be covered with cloth, which was often black crepe.

In World War I, army soldiers who suffered a family death were allowed to wear a black button at the second top on their tunic. This could be done by blackening the brass button, by covering it with black cloth or by wearing a "death head" button which sometimes had a human skull design. For many years the Royal Marines' dress regulations included the option of covering the second button of tunics with black crepe when soldiers were in private mourning.

Buttons were made from the residue of ammunition during and after World War I. These buttons sizzled and melted, however, emitting a pungent odor when a cigarette lighter was put to them.

The compass button, which looked like a regular military button but secretly contained a working compass, saved lives of British, American and Canadian airmen in World War II. To be successful, the development of this button required absolute secrecy. However, just when the button had been perfected and produced on a large scale, a compass button was seen on display in a London shop window. It was found that the firm who made that button had been working on it for a long while, and its appearance at that time was coincidental. The firm was compensated to withdraw the button from the market.

In America during World War II, metal was forbidden to be used for button making because of its essential wartime use. Metal was so scarce that button collectors were asked by police departments to loan back their uniform buttons until the end of the war.

Manufacturers had to use wood and other material that were not needed for the war. Pearls could not be imported from Japan, so Corning Glass adopted new methods of glass-making to supply buttons for clothing manufacturers. Button makers were allowed to use plastics that were nonessential to wartime needs, so plastic novelty buttons became very popular. Lucite scraps left over from making machine-gun turrets were allowed to be used for button making.

In England, clothing made during World War II had to meet the New Austerity specifications. Three buttons on a garment were the maximum number allowed. Each button had to have "CC" on it, which stood for civilian clothing. Unconventional and cheap material was used for buttons there, too. One sweater by a famous designer had buttons made from scouring powder lids.

Tagua nuts from Ecuador were used for World War II buttons because of the shortage of usual materials. The U. S. purchased two and one half million of them. Their usage was stopped, however, when soldiers in trenches discovered that rats like to eat the tagua buttons!

Although there was a shortage of metal buttons for civilians during World War II, it seems there were too many for sailors on the flaps of their U. S. Navy trousers. According to one retired sailor, opening all of those buttons in certain intimate situations became awkward, so sailors on a date and in search of some "action" would fasten only the two top buttons at the upper right and left corners.

There also have been times in the history of the United States when there have too *many* buttons. In the late 1940s, the United States Army had 1,500,000 plastic buttons it didn't know what to do with. At an Army surplus sale 3,000,000 buttons had been rejected and turned over to the Army. The first half of these were used to fill a swamp area near Lester, Pennsylvania. Before the second half could be dumped there, however, the property owners put a stop to it. They wanted Delaware river silt instead of Army buttons on their land.

In another instance, a large stock of left-over campaign buttons from Andrew Jackson's presidential races were restruck and used as military buttons for the state of Virginia. Jackson's campaign slogan had been put on the backs of the buttons, leaving the fronts plain.

Buttons have often impacted the names of regiments and vice-versa. In the 1600s, an English regiment nicknamed "The Mutton Regiment" was sent to Tangiers to Protect England's interests. The regimental button had a lamb on it.

Confederate troops from Missouri and Arkansas were called "Butternuts" because their uniforms were home-dyed with color obtained from butternuts and walnuts. Civilians having loyalties to the South, but living outside the actual South, identified themselves with the Butternuts by using nut shells as buttons. Northerners didn't like such obvious display of rebel sentiment. On at least one occasion, Union soldiers punished people in Iowa by stripping them of their nut shell buttons.

The large brass buttons on some uniforms of the United States Infantry during the Civil War were called "Doughboy" buttons. They got their name because they resembled globs of dough. The infantrymen themselves came to be known as "Doughboys" when the Federal Cavalry humorously coined the term. It was revived in World War I when American soldiers in Europe objected to being called "Sammies" or "Teddies." They preferred "Doughboys."

The uniform buttons worn by the Royal Winnipeg Rifles illustrate an incident in Canadian history in the late 1800s, when there was an Indian uprising. The Rifles fought valiantly, wearing dark uniforms. From that time, the rebels referred to them as those "little black devils." The regiment was evidently proud of this nickname because they had buttons made showing the figure of a running devil holding a trident in one hand.

Until about 1860, people in America regarded any nonmilitary uniform, including the buttons, as "livery," the badge of servitude. Even police refused to wear them until 1844. An English tourist in America in 1868 complained that he couldn't tell the train conductors from the passengers because they all dressed alike. The first description found of conductors' uniforms and railroad buttons was in 1870.

Uniforms other than military have had, and some still have, their own buttons, such as: Boy Scouts, steamship lines, bus drivers, streetcar conductors, airlines, railways, schools, police, fire departments, businesses such as bands, hotels, restaurants, utility companies, department stores, theaters, theatrical companies, private clubs, magazine staffs, and state and government agencies, such as mail carriers.

Button Gluttons
(Buttons in Excess)

The earliest evidence of excessive buttoning is on a 2000 year-old Indian leather gown found in 1865 in the Altai Mountains of western Siberia. Sewed onto the gown are 8000 wooden buttons covered with gold. It was dug from a tomb, having been preserved by frost in which it lay. It now lays in a Moscow museum.

People as a culture have gone "bonkers about buttons" since the French courtiers in the 1200s trimmed themselves lavishly with them. Eventually free-flowing garments were replaced by tighter, more form-fitting clothes. Finer fabrics which wouldn't withstand repeated piercing with pins were introduced, so the buttonhole evolved. Clothes were slit from neck to ankle simply so that a parade of buttons could be used to close it. The slits were often in impractical places—along sleeves and down legs—just so the wearers could display buttons that actually closed. Buttons became status symbols among the wealthy. There could have been as many as 200 closing an outfit, enough to discourage undressing!

In 1284 nobleman Bogo de Clare wore a cloak with six score of coral buttons on it. Children were introduced at young ages to the idea of excessive buttons. In 1273, buttons by the score were bought for the five-year-old Prince Henry, the eldest son of Edward I, his sister, Eleanore and their seven-year-old cousin, John of Brittany. In 1290, Queen Eleanor, wife of Edward I of England, attended her sister's wedding in a dress that was trimmed with 636 silver buttons.

Statues, illustrations and paintings of the 1300s and 1400s attest to button mania. This mania peaked in the 1500s when jewel-studded gold and silver buttons were sewn on clothes merely as decorations, just as buttons were before the creation of buttonholes. Buttons were magnificent gold and silver specimens, indicating the flamboyant fashions of the times. They were costly with the shaping and decorating being done, one at a time, by skilled workmen and artists. Nobility used them to indicate power. In their lust for fancier and fancier buttons, the kings drove the skillful guild button makers to great heights of artistry.

In the first half of the 1500s, King Francis I of France took the fashion of buttons to decorative extremes. He invited the great Italian goldsmith Benvenuto Cellini to Paris to make buttons for him. In 1520, he ordered over 13,000 solid gold buttons set with precious stones from his jeweler, Jacques Polin. He out-buttoned everyone by having all 13,000-plus buttons sewn on a single black velvet court costume. Every seam was lined with buttons. He wore the suit for a summit meeting with King Henry VIII of England. Henry wore jeweled buttons which were patterned after the rings on his fingers. Contemporary historians have described Francis' summit suit as having "resembled a Las Vegas casino when bright lights hit it."

Sometime after the summit meeting, Henry VIII was reputed to have worn a costume decorated with 15,000 buttons sewn on for decoration only in order to out-do Francis. When Henry married his fourth wife, Anne of Cleves, the sleeves of his purple velvet coat were lined with gold and buttoned with diamonds, rubies and pearls from the Orient. Emeralds and other precious stones embellished his girdle, cap and sword.

King Francis I

Button fever spread throughout Europe among the nobility. In 1550, German Emperor Maximilian II wore a black velvet coat trimmed with twenty-four large and fifty-four small, beautifully worked gold buttons. Dandy Veit Konrad Schwarz outdid the King in 1560 by having a quilted woolen jacket made with eight dozen buttons.

Holy Roman Emperor Rudolph II bought buttons in Madrid in sets of fifty-two to sixty in assorted sizes.

In 1583, King Henry III of France had eighteen dozen large silver buttons made in the form of skulls.

An item in the inventory of Mary Queen of Scots stated that in the mid-1500s she had 404 enameled buttons, each with a ruby in the center. She also possessed a gown trimmed with eighty enameled buttons, each set with a pearl.

Queen Elizabeth once received a pair of perfumed gloves with twenty-three small buttons of gold on them, each button hosting a small diamond.

In 1631, Charles Moreau, tailor to the court of King Louis XIII of France, itemized the materials which made up a fine suit. The doublet of silver cloth took sixty buttons of gold and silver thread, and the brown worsted breeches had eighty-four buttons down the side seams.

King Henry III of France

A tailor's bill fifty years later shows an even greater number of buttons on a typical nobleman's suit. The silk coat needed nine and a half dozen gold and silk buttons, and the waistcoat and breeches required four and a half dozen smaller ones.

By 1643, when Louis XIV became King of France, buttons for nobility were used for get-away and ransom purposes, as well as to display wealth and power. Louis got the "button bug" early in his life at age six when a little waistcoat was made for him with thiry-six ruby buttons. He developed a great weakness for buttons and embarked upon a seventy-two-year reign of button buying that cost France over five million dollars, thereby helping to drain the national treasury.

Louis was so laden down with platinum, diamond, ruby and emerald-studded buttons that he couldn't stand up straight. "He sank under the weight of them," wrote French courtier Saint-Simon. One of his vests was buttoned up with buttons worth around $100,000. A costume he wore for dinner with a Persian ambassador reportedly was buttoned and embroidered with twelve million francs' worth of diamonds. The costume was so uncomfortable that the king wore it only a short time, then retired to put on a less weighty outfit.

Button extravagances of French royalty are illustrated by entries in old books like Henry René d'Allemagne's *Les Accessoires du Costume et du Mobilier*. In it is a chronological account of buttons delivered to Louis.

In 1684, he bought 104 buttons, each made of a single diamond. In the same year he had a fifty-two-carat diamond split in two to make a pair of buttons.

In 1685, Louis spent $600,000 for buttons. Records show that he acquired 123 diamond buttons in the month of July alone. One delivery for the king's jacket provided forty-eight buttons of gold, each with a diamond and ninety-six buttonholes, forty-eight of which contained five diamonds and forty-eight with a single diamond.

Among Louis' most sensational button purchases were seventy-seven diamond buttons for over one million dollars.

Louis set the mode for button fashion. Other European rulers did their best to live up to his example. In 1665, the Holy Roman Emperor Leopold I wore a suit made of gold fabric having large diamond buttons. The Elector Maximilian Emanuel of Bavaria bought a set of diamond and ruby buttons for 274,800 florins.

In the Green Vault at Dresden, among the Saxon crown jewels, are sets of buttons that had been made for Augustus the Strong, King of Poland. Included are buttons made with rubies, sapphires, emeralds and topazes. There are thirty coat buttons of rose-cut diamonds.

Sir Walter Raleigh wore pearl and ruby buttons on his clothes. He liked doublets with rows of closely-set jeweled buttons along the edges.

Frederick, first King of Prussia, had eight dozen diamond buttons, each consisting of a large central diamond surrounded by six smaller diamonds. They were worth 5,000 talers. Frederick also had five dozen diamond buttons worth 200 talers apiece. At his coronation in 1701, he wore a scarlet coat stitched in gold and adorned with large diamond buttons worth 3,000 talers.

In the Habsburg Regalia in Vienna in 1731 was a set of thirty-five buttons for a Spanish court dress, each button consisting of a single large brilliant stone and other sets of buttons by the dozen made of sapphires, turquoises, rubies and topazes for coats and waistcoats.

The Archduke Ernest Augustus inherited five dozen flat gold buttons from Emperor Maximilian II, and at his own death left ten dozen crystal buttons and an equal number of other elaborate kinds. Queen Catherine of Poland left five dozen gold buttons, set with rubies and diamonds, valued at 750 pounds sterling, and the Archduke Charles of Styria left 186 Spanish enameled buttons.

George Villiers, the first Duke of Buckingham, often wore clothes for ordinary dancing trimmed with great diamond buttons valued at 80,000 pounds sterling.

Hans Meinhard von Schonberg, a wealthy gentlemen in Germany, owned forty-two gold doublet buttons, each set with seven diamonds.

In the 1700s, King John V of Portugal wore twenty buttons made with famous Brazilian diamonds, each worth at least $20,000, on his state waistcoat.

Earlier in that century, King Louis XV of France favored somewhat sedate engraved gold buttons, perhaps sensing the revolution and not wanting to provoke the people. He had his own boutonnier, though, a servant whose only job was to make buttons.

King Louis XVI who followed in 1774, reverted to the button flamboyance of his grandfather, Louis XIV. His buttons were outlandishly large and ornate, for which he was widely criticized by the philosophers of the day. A note recorded from the 1700s said, "The mania for buttons is today extremely ridiculous. They are of enormous size, some as big as a six-pound crown."

In 1730, the London *Daily Post* reported that King George II had a vastly rich suit, the buttons on his coat being of diamonds, every one worth 250 pounds sterling.

In 1789 in England, Queen Charlotte's gown for the King's birthday had thirty large diamond buttons and tassels fastened on the petticoat.

The English "fops" (young dandies) of the late 1700s were resplendent with jeweled cuff and waistcoat buttons, but they couldn't equal some of the dressers of the previous century.

In the 1700s, button makers pioneered techniques that allowed mass production of buttons, making them accessible to almost everyone, not just a pampered few. Cheap buttons for the lower classes were produced in factories. In the latter part of the 1700s and early part of the 1800s even tradesmen wore coats loaded with innumerable gilt buttons.

Gwendolen Raverat, granddaughter of Charles Darwin, remembered in her book, *Period Piece,* how buttoned-up people at the turn of the nineteenth century were.

> "There must have been something aristocratic about buttons in those days, for everything that could possibly button and unbutton was made to do so: buttons all down the front of one's nightgown, buttons on the sleeves, buttons on one's bodices (the undergarment) and drawers, buttons everywhere. That anonymous genius who discovered that clothe could be slipped over one's head had not yet been born."

Expensive buttons were still made manually by skilled artisans for those who could afford them. King Ludwig II of Bavaria, whose main claim to greatness was his sponsoring of Richard Wagner, once had a costume made of gold cloth, velvet and lace for an appearance in Wagner's opera, "Die Meistersinger." Ten nuns worked for ten years to complete the King's costume, which was embroidered in rich gold and had over 80,000 buttons with eighty seed pearls individually sewn on each button and fourteen smaller buttons. An offer to purchase this costume for $420,000 was made by J. P. Morgan when he visited Germany in 1912. The offer was refused, but the costume was eventually brought to America and placed in the museum collection of the Traphagen School of Fashion in New York City.

From the 1860s to the early 1900s, buttons were so abundant on apparel that people used buttonhooks to get dressed. Shoes had up to twenty-six buttons each, gloves up to twenty-four buttons each; men's jackets often had twenty-one buttons and ladies' dresses could have 100 or more buttons. Little girls' dresses were equally well-buttoned, having as many as eighty-eight. Boys' outfits made up in size what they lacked in numbers.

In 1868, a polonaise (dress with fitted waist) for home wear took three and a half dozen solitaire buttons to complete the accessory details.

In 1879, *Demorest* magazine wrote of buttons painted by competent artists, forty to sixty a dress, with no one button resembling the others.

In 1876, it was fashionable to trim dresses from the throat to the hem of the skirt, the pockets, sleeves, etc. with very small, round flat metal buttons. They were set in series of four, five or six rows, making the wearer look like an exhibitor of coins.

In the early 1900s, fashion's latest fad was a craze for buttons. It seemed to appeal to the vanity of men as much as to women. Waistcoat buttons, each painted separately by well-known miniature painters and framed in silver and gold sometimes cost as much as $100 apiece.

Buttons were used lavishly for clothes decoration in the 1940s. A woman was seen on Fifth Avenue in New York City wearing a dress which had 1800 buttons. On each sleeve there were 100, on the body, basque and collar, 350 and on the skirt, 1350. Those on the skirt were arranged in triangles, stars, squares and other curious shapes on a foundation of black satin. It required a lady of considerable strength to wear it.

Also in the 1940s, a Kansas button enthusiast is said to have sewn more than 6,000 buttons on a muslin cape, using 900 yards of thread.

Another button zealot received a barrel of buttons by express mail weighing 260 pounds. It contained 40,000 buttons from a friend.

Even dolls have been heavily buttoned. At the Florida State Fair in 1937, a doll was exhibited which was wearing a velvet dress with more than 4,000 antique buttons on it. It represented the days of the Southern brides prior to the Civil War when young women wore dozens and dozens of buttons on prewedding party dresses.

Extravagant buttons have been themes for fashion designers since 1945 when Schiaparelli, the noted Parisian designer, used them in all kinds and in great abundance on tailored suits and coats.

In the 1960s, the famous designer Givenchy put copious amounts of buttons on clothes. They ran along sleeves in rows, simulated the buttoning of front and back panels and appeared on tops of skirt panels and at shoulders, much as they did more than a century before.

About the same time, Louis Gottlieb, a button designer for Lidz Brothers had his office covered wall-to-wall with buttons.

In 1987, Paris designer Patrick Kelly featured a hand-sewn wool dress adorned with 3,000 buttons and priced at $15,000.

There are still people who, like earlier kings, are obsessed with buttons and love to display them by the hundreds of thousands. Dalton Stevens, known as the Button King from South Carolina, started covering his belongings with buttons in 1983. He has covered his clothes, shoes, musical instruments, car, outhouse, toilet and his future hearse and coffin with buttons. The hearse has over 600,000 buttons on it.

Mary Diamond, a button collector in California, once had a dress with 5000 buttons on it and a hat with 1000 buttons.

Throughout the twentieth century, the most consistent example of flamboyant buttoning has been that of the Pearly Kings and Queens in London. For the coronation of Queen Elizabeth II, the reigning Pearly King wore a costume covered with 60,000 buttons. It weighed fifty pounds. The last undisputed Pearly King leader died in 1954. His coffin was covered with his 30,000 coat buttons and was carried through London followed by Pearly mourners in their glittering costumes.

Members of the Pearly families continue their pearl-covered costume tradition in London on special holidays and can be seen all together, dressed in full button-covered regalia, on the last Sunday in September when a Pearly Harvest Festival is held at St. Mary-le-Bow Church and another on the first Sunday in October at St. Martins-in-the-Fields.

Buttons That Don't Button
(Names, Places and Things)

Names, places and things have been called buttons for centuries. Sometimes they are named for their relationship or similarity to buttons. Other times they don't have a thing to do with the buttons that fasten or decorate clothes.

Button was a perfectly proper first name in England where Button Gwinnett was born in 1735. He signed the Declaration of Independence, thus putting the word "Button" in the most important document in the United States He was killed in a duel less than a year after signing the Declaration, so his signatures are very valuable to autograph collectors because there are so few of them. In 1957, newspapers across the country had headlines about a $50,000 Button. They were referring to the value of a Button Gwinnett signature.

Button Gwinnett descended from Admiral Sir Thomas Button, an English navigator, who was sent by the King in 1612 to find the Northwest Passage and to rescue the explorer, Henry Hudson. Admiral Button wintered in a sheltered cove on Hudson Bay, which is still called Button Bay.

Nobility and foreign ambassadors who were authorized to attend the hunting events of Napoleon III and Empress Eugenie were called the Buttons. The name came about because these people received a box of buttons from the grand master of the hunt for the decoration of their uniforms and hats.

In Great Britain, Buttons used to be an informal term for page-boys because of the row of buttons fastening their jackets. The *Oxford English Dictionary* refers to examples of this beginning in 1848.

In the pantomime version of "Cinderella," Buttons is the page-boy who proves to be Cinderella's faithful friend in her darkest hour before the fairy godmother steps in to help. The character Buttons was a creation of the pantomime writer J. J. Byron, who introduced him in the classic 1860 version of "Cinderella."

Buttons is also an American cowboy's affectionate word for a boy. The term appears often in Western fiction.

When Lydia Boles became Mrs. Frank Button in 1923 in Vermont, she began to collect buttons. This bit of lore was discovered by Sherry White when she bought two boxes from Mrs. Button's estate; one box contained her collection of over 500 beautiful buttons and the other held her old letters.

Button and Buttons are used for pets' names and as nicknames. President John F. Kennedy's pet name for his young daughter, Caroline, was Buttons.

Associated Press Chief Middle East correspondent Terry Anderson, a hostage for seven years of the Muslim Shiite fundamentalists, wrote a poem called "Button" during his captivity. It was about his daughter, whom he then began calling Button.

Actor Nathan Bexton of "Dangerous Minds" and "Nowhere" has a cat named Buttons.

Larry Button, a service station operator in San Francisco in 1942, omitted his last name on his business card and sewed on a red button instead.

There was a Miss Button Bug crowned at the second California State Button Society's convention in 1944. Hundreds of interesting buttons formed the costume of pretty Miss Virginia Pearce, age sixteen. She succeeded pretty Jacquely Clark, Miss Button Bug, of 1943, who sewed the buttons on Miss Pearce's swimming suit.

In the 1950s, a twelve-year-old boy who collected pinback buttons and covered his cap with them was dubbed Buttonhead by London and American newspapers.

A Yugoslavian rock group in the 1980s was called Bjelo Dugme, which means "White Button."

Dick Button is the name of a two-time Olympic ice skating star. A New York newspaper once ran a headline that said, "Button Is Voted Best Athlete," referring to nineteen-year old Dick Button when he won the James E. Sullivan Memorial Trophy.

While on vacation, well-known button collector, Lucille Weingarten, saw a sign saying "Buttons" by a highway. She was chagrined to find out when she knocked on the door of the nearby house that there were not buttons for sale. The family's name was Buttons.

At one time there was an organization called the Button Brotherhood. A coin-like, gold-plated and hand-engraved medallion exists with the words, "Badge of the Button Brotherhood."

Even periods of time have been named after buttons. In 1949, there was a Button Week in Chicago.

In 1989, button collectors across the United States began celebrating the week of March 13–19 as National Button Week. Button exhibits were organized nationwide. Mayors of some cities signed proclamations designating the week, but it isn't nationally "official" because it hasn't yet been sanctioned by Congress.

In 1968, Governor Harold LeVander proclaimed October 9 as Button Collectors' Day in Minnesota.

Button Day in Australia is the usual name for flag day.

Songs about buttons have been sung since at least 1870 when "Give My Button String to Sister" was published. The song was composed when a child on a sick bed believed she was about to die and asked her mother to "Give my button string to sister, I'll not want it anymore."

Other songs written and popularized about buttons are "The Buttons Are Marked U. S." in 1902, "Button Up Your Overcoat" in 1928 and "Buttons and Bows," which won the Academy Award for best song. The last song was introduced in 1948 by Jane Russell and Bob Hope in the movie, "The Paleface." "Buttons and Bows" sold over a million copies when it was recorded by Dinah Shore.

There is a contemporary movie entitled "The War of the Buttons," which is based upon the French novel "La Guerre des Boutons." The movie tells a story about two gangs of young boys in Ireland. Whenever a member from one gang is captured by the enemy gang, the captive's coat and shirt buttons are cut off with a knife and great ritual. The buttons were the trophies from the battles. A major part of the plot involves one gang's efforts to earn money to keep buying buttons in order to keep its members' dignities.

There is a children's television program in England called "Button Man."

Broadway productions using the button word in their titles are "High Button Shoes" from the 1940s and "Buttons on Broadway" from 1995, starring Red Buttons at age seventy-six.

There are many books of fiction with buttons in their titles. Some use buttons in the story, such as: *The Affair of the Sixth Button* (an Armchair Mystery by Clifford Knight), *Button, Button* (a Crime Club book about murder in a button club by Marion Bromhall), *Mr. Bremble's Buttons* by Dorothy Langley and *Matilda's Buttons* by Mabel Leigh Hunt. Others refer to characters in the book such as *Buttons, the Dog Who Was More Than a Friend* by L. Yeatman. Then there are books that use the word "button" with insinuated meaning in their title such as *A Few Buttons Missing,* an autobiography of a psychiatrist by Fisher and Hawley.

In addition to Button Bay on Hudson Bay in Manitoba, Canada, places with button names include an inlet on Lake Champlain called Buttonmould Bay. The latter was scouted in 1756 by Roger's Rangers and is near the famous spot that Benedict Arnold scuttled the first American Navy to save it from British capture in 1776. Benjamin Franklin, in a letter in 1764, referred to Buttonmould Bay as having been named for the pebbles which were all formed like buttons.

There is a Button Street in Worcester, Massachusetts, and in Bozeman, Montana, and a Button Cemetery near Spring Green, Wisconsin. The cemetery received its name from an early settler by the name of Button who donated the land for the community's first burial ground.

There are four Button Islands, one in the Falkland Islands, one in the Northwest Territory, one off Chile and one in Hingham, Massachusetts. There is a Button Point in Canada, a Button Rock in Tanganyika, a Buttonwood Cap in Honduras, a Buttonwoods in Rhode Island and a Buttonwillow, California.

Knopfkonig Graz is the capital of Styria, a province of Austria. It means "Button King," and the name is used as a backmark on some of the buttons made there.

A felt mill in Boonton, New Jersey, from 1896 to 1923 was known as the button factory because the residents saw barrels and barrels of buttons around it. The felt was made from old clothing, but the buttons were removed first.

Years ago a little haberdashery shop in Harrogate, England, with the name F. Dutton over the door was bought solely to obtain the name. It became the famous Duttons for Buttons.

There is also a shop in New York City called Tender Buttons and in London one called The Button Queen, which was founded by Toni Frith who is personally known as the Button Queen.

Nature abounds with buttons. The buttonwood tree of the sycamore family obtained its name because its fruit looks like round, ball-type buttons, sometimes called buttonballs. Perhaps the most famous such tree is associated with the New York Stock Exchange, which was instituted at 68 Wall Street in 1792 under a buttonwood tree when merchants gathered under it to organize their trading in stocks. The celebrated tree fell in an 1865 storm.

The close-grained yellowish wood of the buttonwood tree is used in the manufacture of buttons. Buttonwood Farm Winery in Solvang, California, gets its name from the buttonwood trees on the property. The winery publishes a newsletter called "The Wooden Button."

There is a buttonweed that grows in the East and southeastern coastal plain, and a buttonbush shrub that has dense, rounded heads simulating buttons.

There is the charming, old-fashioned flower called the bachelor button, and the button snakeroot and rattlesnake-master button snakeroot, which are both members of the parsley family.

There are button mushrooms in our grocery stores and also mescal or peyote buttons, which are the crowns of the hallucinogenic peyote cactus plant that the Aztec Indians used to sun-dry into brown, disc shapes. Plains Indians moistened and ate them during religious ceremonies, and some college students eat them on weekends.

Button stone is the name given to a peculiar kind of slate found in central Germany. It was so named because buttons are made from it in Germany and Sweden.

There are rock formations that are called the Buttons in Bryce Canyon National Park in southwestern Utah.

Button quails are birds from the Turnicidae family that resemble quails but lack a hind toe.

The spots on an American Curl breed of cats are called "buttons."

Perhaps the most common button in nature was brought to the attention of Lucille Weingarten, when she asked a flea-market dealer if he had any buttons. "Yes, I've got one button," he said, as he pulled up his T-shirt to show her his belly button!

The word "button" has been used to name an invention. The skin button, invented by Dr. Benedict Daly, is a circular device made of a porous material which prevents skin from growing closed, allowing drip drugs and nutrients into the body. The skin button remains infection-free for months.

Edible buttons found their way into the U. S. market beginning when General Mills marketed a snack product called Buttons, which was inspired by the song "Buttons and Bows."

In the 1970s, candy called Jujubees in the shape of four-holed sew-threw buttons were sold in stores.

Buttons That Don't Button

In the early 1990s, Farley's advertised a candy called Choc-o-buttons, which were button-shaped chocolate.

Necco candy buttons are packaged with a series of pre-school children's books called "Nibble Me Books." By eating the correct candy buttons while reading the stories, children learn basic concepts like colors, counting and following instructions.

Button candies are quite popular in England. The Fudge Company in England makes Tasty Toffee Buttons; Cadbury Land makes Dairy Milk Buttons; and Marks and Spencer sells White Chocolate Buttons.

Also in England, a bachelor's button is a small biscuit. Dorset Knob buttons, made from sheeps' horn, muslin and linen thread, originated in the late 1600s in Dorset, England. The famous and delicious Dorset Knob bisuits are named after Dorset Knob buttons.

Culinary buttons that weren't commercially successful were Mutton Buttons. These chocolate-filled shortbread cookies were packaged in boxes showing a sheep who said, "Ewe'll love them." Mutton Buttons are one of the 65,000 marketing failures in a museum called New Products Showcase and Learning Center in Ithaca, New York.

Cooks all over can make their own button cookies by decorating regular icebox cookies with shredded coconut, sliced orange peel or frosting put on to look like thread sewn through the "button."

Martha Stewart advocates making them by using any recipe for rolled cookies that hold their shapes and making the button shapes with a round cookie cutter. The inner ring is added by gently pressing the rim of a glass, slightly smaller than the cookie, into the dough. The four holes can be made with a skewer before baking.

Buttons are also used for various kinds of identification purposes. There used to be bottle buttons that were made by stamping pieces of molten glass and applying them to cooling bottles. These became markers identifying merchants and dates of bottling.

The button knot is a small round knot acting as a button. The buttonhole stitch is a reinforced looped sewing technique used for the edge of material. There are several variations, such as the tailor's buttonhole stitch used for buttonholes and the open type used to finish blanket edges.

A button tow is a kind of ski lift for one person consisting of a pole that has a circular plate at the bottom and is attached to a moving cable.

One type of organ is called a button chord organ.

A door button in England is a button with which a door is closed or a coat is fastened.

In days gone by, a peace or mortgage button was a knob, often made of wood or metal on a post of a stairway. It meant that the house was paid for, that the owner and contractor were "at peace." An example of this old New England custom exists in Alton, New Hampshire, in the Lea-Davis House where Abraham Lincoln stayed as a guest many times. The newel post is inlaid with a plain ivory button symbolizing the house is paid for, free and clear.

Chinese Mandarins, the civil and military officials, used to wear distinctive balls on their funnel-shaped hats to indicate rank. Rank was identified by the color of these buttons. Civilian mandarins of the highest rank had a ruby-colored button; the second was coral red; the third was sapphire; the fourth was purple; the fifth was crystal; the sixth was jadestone; the seventh was embossed gold; the eighth was plain gold; the ninth was silver.

Men who passed examinations to hold office but who had not yet received their appointments, wore buttons of appropriate color but smaller size.

On firemen's uniforms throughout the United States, collar buttons indicate the wearer's rank. One bugle means lieutenant, two upright bugels are for captain, two crossed bugels mean battalion chief, three bugels signify deputy chief and five bugels designate chief.

Bridle buttons (called bridle rosettes) don't button, although they are often found in button boxes. They are constructed with square shanks that fasten into the headstalls on horses' bridles. They were used for ornamentation on horses' bridles as early as Alexander the Great's time in the mid 300s BCE. Their use became widespread beginning around 1800, and they remained popular until World War I. They were also used on camels and camel caravans in Iran in the 1940s. Their method of construction was similar as that of clothes buttons.

Like dress and uniform buttons, bridle rosettes were made of all mentionable materials of their day. Some had flowers, animals, monograms, fraternal and commercial emblems, horseshoes, coats of arms and even jewels. Pictures of people and pets under glass were popular after the 1870s. American Indians made them in turquoise and silver.

Bridle rosettes attached to the harnesses of horses in England in the 1800s were supposed to ward off evil, advertise the occupation or profession of the owner and bring good luck.

After the Civil War, the first order chartered by Congress involved bridle buttons. Bridle rosettes with the letters FCB on the emblem (standing for friendship, charity and benevolence), were ordered by the United States Congress to engender a friendlier feeling between the North and the South.

There are several types of buttons that don't button but rather are pinned or sewn onto fabrics or objects for purposes other than fastening. Stud buttons have held clothes together, but many have been used solely for decoration by means of eyelets called stud holes. They are sometimes called lapel buttons.

Women, as well as men, wore stud buttons as evidenced by the wedding gifts that Princesses Helena, Louisa and Victoria gave the Princess Royal of England when she married the Crown Prince of Russia in 1856. Each princess gave a massive gold stud button, ornamented with pearls, emeralds, rubies and sapphires.

Some of the lapel buttons, such as the ferrotype portraits of presidential candidates in 1860, had brass rims with a hole through them to hold ribbons which were then inserted and attached to the lapel.

Members of the Thirteen Club, formed in 1882 with chapters in New York and London, were required to wear on their lapels small coffins from which a tiny skeleton dangled. Meetings were held on the thirteenth of each month because of triskaidekaphobia, which is the fear of the number thirteen. Members engaged in various fate-tempting antics to show their disdain for superstitions.

In more contemporary times, lapel buttons served a clandestine purpose for Freemasons in Germany. In the 1930s after Hitler's rise to power, masonry was forced underground. The Masons used lapel buttons in the shape of forget-me-not flowers on them as their means of identification.

There were buttons advertised in 1886 called electric sleeve buttons, which were a type of stud button. They were animated novelty buttons from France. Some had dancing girls under glass. The little dolls were made out of paper. The doll's arms, legs and head were attached by wire springs to the torso. Their faces and hair were drawn in ink, and they wore little dresses made of colored foil with gold or black paint embossed along the necklines and waists. Every movement of the hands set the figure quivering. They went through all movements known to ballerinas. People said watching them was almost as good as going to the theater.

There were also electric moving figures of bugs, turtles, horses and dice buttons where the dice were so perfect that games could be played with them on their little green felt backgrounds. There were working roulette wheels made of multicolored paper with small escutcheons in the centers. A tiny ball rolled around when the stud was moved. Another design had a thermometer under glass, attached to a bright brass background. Engraved on the brass were both the Fahrenheit and Celsius scales. Another design had a jiggly skeleton.

Some of the early campaign buttons were lapel buttons. One such button was a mechanical button in the Cleveland-Blaine campaign in 1884. It was shaped in the form of Cleveland's standing profile. When the heel of the shoe was pressed, out popped Cleveland's arm in the position of thumbing his nose.

By 1880, there were more campaign lapel buttons than campaign clothing buttons. In 1896, celluloid pin-back buttons made their appearance and have since outnumbered all other types of political memorabilia.

Places, too, have used nonshank buttons to advertise. The American Museum of Natural History in Manhattan gave out little white clip metal buttons with a picture of a dinosaur to people who paid admission.

A distant cousin, the pin-back button, emerged in the late 1800s. Although they are really pins, their use and purpose closely parallels that of lapel buttons. Early pin-backs were made by button manufacturers, and pin-backs have always been called buttons by the newspapers, button trade magazines and sales people.

Celluloid pin-back buttons made their first appearances as campaign buttons during the presidential campaigns of the late 1800s. Every four years since that time, pin-backs have appeared as advertising gimmicks for presidential campaigns.

A two-inch campaign button of Grover Cleveland showed a chair with the words, "Who Shall Occupy It?" on the front. When a small clasp on the bottom of the chair was released, the seat popped up and Cleveland's picture was shown.

The penchant for socially unacceptable messages was more or less accepted on pin-backs since their early days in the 1890s. One showed a pig with a hole at its rear end. When someone looked through the hole, a picture of Benjamin Harrison appeared. Another in 1960 said, "YCERSOYA—You Can't Elect Republicans Sitting On Your Ass." There have been many more derogatory buttons not suitable for print.

An example of a mechanical pin-back button was the Panic Button in 1964 on a campaign button for Barry Goldwater. When a red button was pressed, a flag flew into view reading, "Vote for Goldwater."

The largest pin-back button ever used for campaigning was nine inches in diameter and was from the Franklin Roosevelt campaign in 1941. It said, "A Pauper of Roosevelt." Another pin back for that campaign said, "We Want Beer."

Pin-back buttons were often made of celluloid until 1944. Because the materials used for celluloid were required for war work, pin-backs were then made of enameled tin, leather, cloth and plastics.

The use of buttons for advertising was broadened tremendously by pin-backs. They have touted everything in food products and services. In 1896, the Sweet Caporal Cigarette Company pinned a free celluloid pin-back button on every pack of cigarettes. Pictures of actresses, sports figures, flags, flowers, birds, sovereigns, state seals, ships, animals and comics were the subjects of these buttons. Other tobacco companies copied the gimmick and used pin-backs prolifically. In 1964, a red button that said, "I'm Particular" was introduced to sell Pall Mall cigarettes. The buttons were in so much demand that the initial order of 150,000 buttons was increased to one million.

Another pin-back advertised the drink, No-Cal. People could order the button for ten cents, and more than 6,000 sent for it.

The Avis Company at one time gave away more than two and a half million pin-backs which said, "We Try Harder."

During World War I, there was a series of pin-back buttons called the Liberty Loan Series, and during World War II there were patriotic pin-backs that used letters of various patriotic organizations such as NRA and USO.

Through the years many companies and organizations have used pin-back buttons for advertising and propaganda. Red Cross, Community Chest, War Bonds, religious organizations and lodges are examples.

In 1953 in New York City, saucer size pin back buttons welcoming guests to the city became a union issue between bellhops who had to wear them and the Governor Clinton Hotel management.

In 1965, there were six different buttons honoring Pope Paul's VI visit to New York. Button sizes were from one and three-fourths inches to six inches. "Street hawkers" sold the buttons at one dollar each at Yankee Stadium, St. Patrick's Cathedral, the United Nations and all along the route traveled by His Holiness. "Hey, Hey!" they shouted, "Honor the Holy Father. Get your Pope button here."

Pin-back buttons have been popular with all age groups. When nine-year old David Bittner heard Rose Kennedy speak in Nebraska during the Kennedy-Nixon campaign, he was already a Democrat. At the rally, a man handing out Kennedy buttons refused to give David one, however, because he was too young to vote. A few days later David's father gave him a big white pin-button that said, "If I were 21, I'd vote for Kennedy."

In a 1998 Ann Landers column, a pin-back button solved "Cheerful in California's" problem of being bombarded with tiresome questions after she had broken her arm. "Cheerful" had a button made to wear on her sling that read, "I fell and broke my arm. So, how was YOUR summer?" She felt the ensuing laughter from people contributed to the healing.

Pin-backs have remained popular and inexpensive tools for advertising through the present, although money spent on them lessened considerably when bumper stickers became popular in the 1970s.

Buttons nowadays that reflect current events are often in pin-back form. In addition to political and campaign issues, they commemorate special events and social causes like moon landings, civil rights struggles, the war on poverty and women's liberation. Slogans appear on them saying, "Praise the Pill," "I Fight Poverty, I Work," and "Ban the Bra."

Pin-backs are worn by people as silent reminders of great events and endorsements of people, issues and products.

Outlaw Buttons
(Button Laws)

In his magazine, "All Year Round," Charles Dickens wrote about buttons, "... perhaps no single article of commerce has been made more account of by the legislature. The button world has been ruled and regulated like a pampered child, and acts and bills by the dozen have been passed, ordering what kinds of buttons should be worn, and what kinds discarded . . ."

In the mid-1200s, King Louis IX of France issued a royal decree making ornamental buttons the mark of aristocracy. The lower classes, clerks and any class below, were not allowed to wear metal buttons; they were restricted to cloth or thread-covered ones.

A church council also banned the use of gold, silver or other metallic buttons by clerks, thus further establishing a class distinction between the nobility and the commoner, according to the buttons worn.

Henry III of England followed with a law forbidding "artificers, artisans, tradesmen and yeomen" the wearing of buttons other than those made of pewter, bone or wood.

The French laws governing buttons in the 1200s were from *The Book of Trades* by Étienne Boileau. The King appointed Étienne Boileau as Provost of Paris, a position which functioned rather like a mayor today. The laws governing French craft guilds were similar to today's unions.

The production of buttons was strictly controlled by this guild. There was a long list of requirements, all of which commanded fines to be paid to the king and the forfeiture of buttons if the requirements were not met. No button maker could have more than one apprentice who had to be born in "honest" wedlock. The apprentice had to pay a tenth of his wages to the king. A button maker's workday finished when the town crier announced the time in the evenings. There were strict regulations regarding what type of buttons each button maker could make. Except when his wife was in childbirth, a button maker had to take turns at watchman's duty. A jury of eleven men was appointed by the Provost to enforce the rules and inflict penalties upon those who disobeyed them. These and other harsh laws were in effect up to the French Revolution.

Later in the 1200s in England, Henry III made it unlawful for the poor to wear buttons covered with rich materials, such as cloth of gold, silver, satin and silk. The wealthy and nobles wore them, and the poor wore coarse homespun buttons.

In the 1300s, a French law was passed declaring that only goldsmiths were allowed to make buttons of gold or other precious metals. Brass or copper buttons were made only by manufacturers called boutonniers, and only rosary makers could fashion buttons from bone or ivory.

The ordinary people began to copy the styles of the court fashions. Many laws were drawn up in the 1300s and 1400s to curtail extravagance among the middle class, but the laws were difficult to enforce. In his book, *The Medici,* George Frederick Young told how the magistrates of Renaissance Italy underestimated the power of button-loving women when they tried to outlaw the wearing of fine buttons. In the 1400s, the women fought vigorously in numerous ways and waged an untiring warfare with the officials in charge of enforcing the sumptuary laws.

In an official record in Florence, Italy, administrator Giovanni di Bicci wrote a report that described one of his men attempting to enforce a button law: "Then going further he findeth one wearing many buttons in front of her dress, and he saith to her, 'Ye are not allowed to wear these buttons.'

"But she answers, 'These are not buttons but studs, and if ye do not believe me, look . . . they have no loops, and moreover there are no buttonholes.'"

The authority remarked, "We do but knock our heads against a wall."

In the 1500s, people took so little notice of the button laws that Henry VIII of France reaffirmed the law in 1550 and increased the penalties. It was, however, a futile attempt. Legislation could not alter the desire of people to wear the buttons they wanted.

In Elizabethan England, however, there were laws actually forcing certain classes to wear buttons. Household servants were fined for such infractions as a shirt missing a button. The fine was six pence. That was a severe penalty, amounting to about two days' pay. The money was deducted from wages and given to the poor.

Miniature portrait buttons used to depict facial features and clothing that were perfect in detail. A Spanish or Italian court artist painted miniatures of King Henry IV of France and his mistress, Henriette De Blazac, using a jeweler's glass. Such artists ruined their eyes doing the close work, so a court ban was put on the practice. Now it's a lost art.

In the 1600s, legislation regulating the use of richly covered buttons was passed again; only the gentry could wear them. All through the 1600s, there was a succession of button laws. King Charles II of England protected home button making, not by tariffs, but by prohibition and heavy fines for selling or wearing foreign-made buttons. The penalty was 100 pounds sterling for the importer and 50 pounds sterling for the seller.

In 1693, King William III and Queen Mary II continued the imported-button prohibition. Around this time, covered buttons made of the same material as the garment on which they were worn came into style. These were supplied by tailors. The makers of silk-embroidered buttons protested and convinced Parliament that many thousands of men, women and children depended upon the making of silk, mohair, gimp and thread-buttons with needles and would be unemployed if cloth-covered buttons were legal. Parliament issued a royal declaration forbidding anyone to make, sell or wear cloth-covered buttons. There was a penalty of forty shillings for every dozen cloth-covered buttons sold or put on garments. The fancy button makers were given the right to search shops and homes for illegal buttons. Fines and confiscations were frequent. People were arrested on the streets.

Also in the 1600s, the Button Makers Guild in France raised a cry of outrage because tailors made buttons out of cloth. The government imposed a fine on the cloth button makers and on those who wore cloth buttons. The Button Guild members were allowed to search people's homes and wardrobes and arrest them on the streets, just as in England, if they were seen wearing the subversive buttons.

France at this time also prohibited the use of metal buttons to protect the Lyons and Paris silk industries. The needle workers who provided silk buttons found their wares losing popularity. In 1694, King Louis XIV helped the industry by making buttons other than silk illegal for ordinary citizens. To manufacture buttons of any material except silk was a crime punishable by a fine of 500 livres, of which two-thirds went to the informant. Jewelers and goldsmiths made elaborate buttons for the Court. Later the King protected the handicraft of needlework buttons still further by forbidding the covering of buttons with loom-woven silk.

King Louis XIV also decreed that embroiderers in the lacemakers' guild could make buttons of every shape and fabric as long as they did not "combine artificial with genuine material."

Many of these button laws in both England and France were soon appealed and abandoned because of the difficulties in enforcing them.

The United States had button legislation in the 1600s in Connecticut where anyone who wore gold or silver buttons was taxed.

There were other European laws from this time period pertaining to buttons. One in the late 1600s had to do with button-making machines in England. Some of them were being used to make coins instead of buttons. Parliament examined all of these machines and revoked several licenses.

Before the mid-1600s at Oxford University, the social status of people was evident by the buttons they wore. When it became impossible to tell the status from buttons, the University attempted to solve the problem with button rules. In 1666, the rules were printed for the tailors in English and for the scholars in Latin: Servants were to wear no buttons. (Many students brought their own servants.) The commoner's gown was to have six buttons on each sleeve, not to cost more than five shillings and not to be bigger than the public patterns. A gentlemen commoner could wear four dozen buttons, same price and size as above. A baronet and knight could also wear four dozen buttons on each sleeve, but they could be of gold or silver.

Until the early part of the 1700s in England, regulation stipulated who could wear which type of button and designated its composition materials. Only nobles and a few of the wealthiest merchants were allowed to wear buttons of precious materials. Other social classes were required to wear buttons of bone, wood or handspun fabric.

In France also, class distinction was made by material used in buttons. The commoners were required to use coarse thread. The aristocracy were allowed gold and silver thread and sequins, precious and semiprecious stones.

At the beginning of the 1700s, Queen Anne of England decreed that no tailor or other person could make, sell or bind any cloth-covered buttons. Anne was followed by George I who passed very stringent laws against cloth-covered buttons in order to encourage the metal button trade. Heavy fines of forty shillings per dozen were imposed on tailors using covered buttons on garments. The law further stated that the person who made or sold the garments should not receive payment if the wearer refused to pay him.

This last part of the law was tested when a tailor named Mr. Shirley sued a Mr. King for nine pounds sterling due for a suit of clothes. Mr. King pleaded nonliability on the grounds of illegal transaction because the buttons on the suit were made of cloth instead of brass. The judge ruled in favor of Mr. King. The most remarkable feature of this case was that the judge, the barrister and the client who profited by it were all buttoned in cloth buttons!

Outlaw Buttons

A similar case tried in the 1770s was ruled in favor of the defendant. In addition, this time the court concurred that if the defendant chose to sue the tailor, the tailor would have to pay forty shillings for every dozen buttons illegally sewn on by him.

In 1721, an act of Parliament was passed to encourage buttons and buttonholes made of silk and mohair.

George II implemented a law to protect the workers of the needle-wrought button, as opposed to the loom-woven button. This law allowed the beautiful hand wrought Dorset-type buttons to be legally made.

In 1737 in Macclesfied, silk button makers rioted against a man who made woven buttons. Woven buttons were eventually exempt from the law prohibiting covered buttons.

As late as 1790, tailors who used cloth buttons were liable for a penalty of five pounds sterling for each dozen, and every person wearing them could be ordered to pay two pounds sterling for each button.

These laws did not discourage the making and use of cloth-covered buttons to any great degree. It is suspected that the fines were paid and itemized as expenses of the businesses. The laws did, however, allow the common man to legally dress up his clothes with more ornate, metal buttons.

Toward the end of the 1790s, the practice of selling illegally covered buttons was prevalent. There were penalties for selling them, but the buttons were sold in spite of the penalties. In *A Century of Birmingham Life,* J. A. Longford wrote this about illegal buttons in 1791:

> "A tradesman in London was fined last week nearly 26 pounds sterling on two informations for selling these articles . . . if any person or persons will give information against such a Wearer or Wearers, so that such Wearer or Wearers shall be convicted thereof, he or they shall upon such Conviction be handsomely rewarded."

In the late 1700s in Britain, any person putting false marks on gilt buttons or erasing any marks except the ones expressing the true quality of the buttons, forfeited the buttons and incurred a penalty of five pounds sterling for any quantity not exceeding twelve dozen and if more than twelve dozen, one pound sterling for every twelve dozen.

It was also unlawful at this time to import foreign buttons.

The makers of papier mâché buttons in the late 1700s referred to the strips of paper panels as "button boards" as as to avoid paying taxes which were levied on the sale of paper and paper goods.

With the beginning of the 1800s, modern covered buttons were born. The Queen Anne, George I and George II laws were voided to meet the tightening foreign trade competition. Instead of laws, creative ideas were encouraged and patents for them were issued.

In the early 1800s, there were no tariffs on buttons that were imported into England. France had only one regulation, and it was a blanket rate for only certain kinds of buttons.

On the death of George III in 1820, orders for the mourning of the Court were posted. Gentlemen were ordered to wear black cloth without buttons on the sleeves and pockets.

In 1830, instead of appealing that Parliament decree button laws, the gilt button makers petitioned King William IV to wear brass-covered gilt buttons rather than silk-covered buttons. The King accepted a richly gilt set and for awhile the dukes and nobility ordered their suits to be decorated with gilt, but the gilt button's popularity declined when Victorian fashions emerged.

Attempts to legislate buttons and who could wear them have diminished since the Victorian period. From time to time, however, some button laws have been imposed. For instance, in wartime in the twentieth century, England enforced clothes rationing and restricted the number of buttons on a shirt to four. Buttonholes were also regulated.

However, indirect attempts to control buttoning were still made. The Men's Dress Reform Party, an English organization, declared war on the collar button in the late 1920s. The aim of this society was "to make clothing less ugly, less unhealthy and less cumbersome." The Reverand W. R. Inge, the "gloomy dean" of St. Paul's Cathedral and one of the founders of the organization, was of the opinion that poplin shorts and tennis shirts made an ideal attire for a business man. The adoption of such a costume would have ended the collar button. This reform was obviously one reform that the Party wasn't able to make.

Until the 1800s there were only a few button manufacturers in the United States. New life was given to the American button manufacturers when a thirty percent tariff was put on imported buttons in 1842.

In the 1830s, country peddlers like William McCoy carried buttons all over southern New England. Many of these buttons were "black market buttons" because the peddlers did not have proper licenses to sell them. On a lithograph of Mr. McCoy holding a basket overflowing with cards of buttons was this poem:

> "Now, good people all,
> Both short and tall,
> Just listen to my ditty,
> And I'll tell you a thing or two
> About Providence City.
> I have buttons, but you can't buy,

Just listen to me and I'll tell you why.
Because by this time you'll all know well,
I have no license here to sell.
And, now, gentlemen, believe what I say,
I shall sell you no more, but give them away;
I charge a nine-pence for my talking,
And throw my buttons in for nothing."

In 1876 in the United States, import duties on most buttons and molds of all kinds were still thirty percent. The exceptions were for barrel buttons used for tassels or ornaments which were fifty cents per pound plus fifty percent, cloth woven buttons which were ten percent, silk cloth which were sixty percent and glass which were forty percent.

In the 1960s, button blanks were imported into the United States, and the holes drilled after they arrived. This way, the buttons were subject to thirty-six percent duty instead of forty percent.

In the 1940s in America, the War Production Board decided that buttons could be saved by leaving them off the places on work pants where suspenders were attached. Lumberjacks, shipyard workers and fishermen protested that if buttons were being saved, it was at the expense of human dignity. A new WPB. order was issued that required buttons on work pants.

In 1952 in England, as preparations for Queen Elizabeth's coronation were being made, the Keeper of the Privey Purse ruled firmly that the Queen's head was not to be depicted on buttons. Most firms canceled tooling and plans for such buttons. However, there were a couple of firms who continued. Their activity was not classified as illegal, but it was regarded as being in poor taste. Several of London's big department stores had the "poor taste" to stock them.

Private twentieth-century institutions have also attempted to regulate buttons, such as Harvard University when it mandated that coat buttons had to be the color of coats on which they were worn, or they had to be black.

Buttons have been the subject of lawsuits, such as the legal action that the Steiff company took when it forced its rivals to stop putting buttons in the ears of the rivals' teddy bears. The rival companies had to move the buttons to other parts of the bears' bodies. Steiff had copyrighted the 'Button in Ear' trademark in 1905.

 In 1964, an enterprising button maker found a way to avoid paying licensing royalties to the Beatles even though he sold Beatle music buttons. He used a rebus design on brass buttons showing a beetle (bug type) and a music note.

Throughout the history of buttons, there have been subcultures who have enforced their own laws regulating buttons. In the 1600s, the Mennonites wore no buttons because of the old-fashioned use of bones to make buttons. This religious sect positively did not believe in killing animals, and all the buttons in the Alps at that time were made from bones of slaughtered animals.

The Mennonites have tolerated buttons since the 1920s. The restrictions against them at that time were broken down at the church's annual conference in 1926. After a week's debate, the older and stricter generation yielded to youthful demands and consented to "countenance buttons for the sake of tolerance" even though they still feared the moral consequences of wearing them.

The Amish people, an off-shoot of the Mennonites in the late 1600s, also rejected buttons because providing bone for the buttons caused the death of animals. In addition, they considered buttons too ornamental and militaristic. Therefore, they rejected all buttons and used only hook and eye fasteners or pins.

The Amish, like the Mennonites, have softened their laws regarding buttons. Between 1870 and 1880, the Amish people in Pennsylvania allowed their daughters limited wear of buttons. In 1960, no buttons were worn by women, but the men were allowed to wear four buttons on their trousers. These were of the plainest and cheapest types. Children were also allowed continued limited use of buttons.

As far back as the 1500s, Puritans rebelled against the increasing magnificence of buttons. Many used hook and eye fastenings in protest. By the 1600s, the Puritans in England revolted and shunned buttons completely. Buttons were also banned from the fashion world in colonial America. The Puritans considered buttons a vulgar display, and anyone who wore them was brought before the church council for correction.

Reform groups like the Quakers and Puritans continued to fight against the showiness and extravagance of the gilt buttons in the early 1800s.

Various subcultures today still regard buttons, especially fancy ones, to be vanities but actual laws prohibiting them are not common.

Literary Buttons
(Buttons in Literature)

Fiction writers have used buttons for descriptive purposes, to show emotion and clarify situations, to add richness and shading to characterizations and to further plots. Even diarists and biographers throughout history have expressed themselves by the usage of button expressions, analogies and symbolisms.

One of the first mentions of buttons in literature was made in *Piers Plowman,* written in 1377. The author told of a knife ornamented with buttons. Jean Froissart, historian and poet, also wrote descriptively about "botones of sylver and gylte" in his work.

When William Shakespeare wrote, "For the apparel oft proclaims the man," he was referring to the art of characterization. By describing the dress of their characters, masters of fiction have told us much about the inner qualities of their characters.

Shakespeare surely did so with buttons in his plays written in the late 1500s and early 1600s. The word "button" appeared five times. The words "buttoned" and "buttonhole" were used once each. Shakespeare also used buttons symbolically. In *Love's Labour's Lost,* a page said to his master, "Let me take you a button-hole lower." The statement suggests the unfastening of the doublet, but there are other implications. It can be interpreted to mean that the two characters should speak casually, or it could be that the servant thinks his master is too conceited.

Another servant in the *Comedy of Errors* said after the arrest of his master, "A devil in an everlasting garment hath him, One whose hard heart is buttoned up in steel."

Laertes said in *Hamlet*:
"The canker galls the infants of the spring
Too oft before their buttons be disclos'd,"

Shakespeare experts think the buttons refer to plant buds, which was a common term, the infants of spring refers to young plants and the canker to a worm. The passage is a warning to Ophelia for her to stay away from Hamlet.

Also from *Hamlet* was, "On fortune's cap, we are not the very button." The button here could mean the chunky peak of the cap, although another interpretation implies that it means they were at the middle of the social ladder. This second opinion is based on the custom of Chinese Mandarins who wore hat buttons to denote their station in life.

In *The Merry Wives of Windsor,* the Host of the Garter Inn said, "Tis in his buttons, he will carry it." This could mean that he will succeed, or it could be a reference to bachelor button flowers that were used to predict success in love.

From *Romeo and Juliet,* the phrase, ". . . he duels expertly enough to be a very butcher of a silk button," means he is accurate with his sword.

In *King Lear,* a button plays a part in the tragic climax of the play. The dying King says:
"Never, never, never, never, never!
Pray you undo this button."

The great novelists of the 1800s frequently incorporated buttons into their stories. Charles Dickens was personally, as well as professionally, keenly interested in buttons. As a reporter and publisher, he wrote articles on buttons and their manufacture in Birmingham. In "Household Words" he wrote about buttons, "There is surely something charming in seeing the smallest thing done so thoroughly, as if to remind the careless that whatever is worth doing is worth doing well." In the same publication, Dickens wrote that scenes on buttons were, "as vivid and faithful as if the designers were busy on a wine-cup for a king."

Dickens used buttons profusely in his novels, too. In the *Pickwick Papers,* he told of the Pickwick Club Button, describing a gilt button which showed Mr. Pickwick and the letters P. C. on either side. ". . . the stranger surveyed himself with great complacency in a cheval glass—the first that's been made with our Club button." In the same book, buttons were used descriptively. There were: a man who wore a coarse striped waistcoat with black calico sleeves and blue glass buttons, a man in a brown coat and bright "basket buttons," Master Tammy Bardell's brass buttons of "considerable size," Mr. Pickwick's wide-shirted green coat with brass buttons and "thunder and lightning" buttons worn by Jack Hopkins.

"Thunder and lightning" button from Charles Dickens' *Pickwick Papers.*

There were many other descriptive button phrases in Dickens' novels, such as those in *Dombey and Son.* Captain Sol Gills wore "basket buttons" and Commander Bundy wore massive wooden buttons like "Back Gammon men." Mr. Dombey himself wore buttons that "sparkled phosphorescently in the feeble rays of the fire."

In *The Christmas Stories,* Dr. Marigold says, ". . . if I have a taste of personal jewellry it is mother-of-pearl buttons."

In *David Copperfield,* little Emily speaks of her Uncle Daniel Peggotty, "If I ever was to be a lady, I'd give him a sky blue coat with diamond buttons."

Robert Graves told his readers in *Goodbye to All That* something about his character's appearance when he said, ". . . I had not only gone to an inefficient tailor, but also had a soldier-servant who neglected to polish my button . . ."

Buttons help describe the scene in *Book of Snobs* by William Thackeray: "Here too, he displayed his hooks, knives and other gardening irons, his whistles, and his strings of spare buttons."

Dickens and Shakespeare both cleverly used buttons for more than mere description. In *David Copperfield* when Peggotty's buttons burst from her dress to all corners of the room as she hugged David Copperfield, Dickens increased the poignancy of the scene by using buttons. In the same novel, he again used buttons to good effect when he showed the stiff formality of a lawyer "whose close fitting drab trousers seemed to button all the way up outside his legs from his boots to his hips." Dickens showed how the man could not turn naturally, being so buttoned up.

In *Oliver Twist,* buttons helped to characterize Mr. Bumble. ". . . You know, dear me, what a very elegant button that is, Mr. Bumble!" said the undertaker.

"Yes, I think it is rather pretty," said the beadle, glancing proudly downwards at the large brass buttons which embellished his coat. "The die is the same as the parochial seal—the good Samaritan healing the sick and bruised man. The board presented it to me on New Year's Morning . . ."

In his poem "A Little Bronze Button," John Parker shows through a button the proudness his character feels about the army:

"The little brown button
The Sacred bronze button
The Grand Army button
He wears ozn his coat."

Another example of an author using buttons to characterize was in *Rumpole on Trial* by John Mortimer: "Don't expect Swabey's ever got near enough to see a fox. He comes out with a string on his tip hat!" Pippa said.

"And a red coat when no one's asked him to wear such a thing," Gavin added to the indictment.

"No, darling. That's not the point. The point is, a red coat with *flat buttons*." And Pippa turned to Hilda for support. "Imagine that, Mrs. Rumpole!"

"Oh, dear. Of course. Flat buttons! How very extraordinary." My wife did her best to sound appalled, while I asked in all innocence, "You mean you'd prefer them *round*?"

"Flat, shiny buttons without a hunt crest on them," Gavin explained. "Means he just got the thing off the peg at Moss Bros."

"Is that a serious offense? I'd never heard of the crime of *flat buttons* before."

Some authors have used buttons simultaneously as both descriptive and characterization vehicles. One such passage is from a "Connoisseur Weekly" magazine: "The rough country squire . . . even the buttons on his clothes are impressed with the figures of dogs, foxes, stages and horses."

Another example is from *Hornblower and the Atropos* by C. S. Forester: "The Lieutenant of the watch . . . wore spotless and unwrinkled white trousers; the buttons on his well-fitting coat winked in the sunshine."

In *The Black Rose*, Thomas Costain not only describes his character, but tells us something about her station in life through her usage of buttons. "Wulfa had dressed her in a flowing gown of green samite, with roses diapered on the bodice. To conceal its age, buttons had been sewn from wrists to elbow in what was the latest fashion."

In another passage, Costain uses buttons to describe a dashing young gypsy in addition to hinting at the gypsy's aspirations: "He was most elaborately attired, a cluster of shilling pieces serving as buttons on his purple-braided maroon coat and pennies fairly rattling on his bright waistcoat. It was clear that he was aping the royal manner of the great gypsies, some of whom wore Spanish gold pieces for back buttons and spaded guineas and half guineas on their coats."

In *Pirate Laureate; The Life and Legend of Captain Kidd,* Willard Hallam Booner described a treasure with silver buttons in it and referred to a character's waistcoat as having been decorated with valuable buttons that later turned out to be "stones of low degree."

There are many examples in literature where buttons have been used for purely descriptive purposes. In *Lark Rise to Candleford,* Flora Thompson says, "Miss Lane once said that she longed to take a needle and thread and set forward the top button of his trousers, so that he could button in the bulge at his waist."

In the famous poem by Albert Gorton Greene, buttons help to describe Old Grimes:

> "Old Grimes is dead; that good old man
>   We never shall see more:
> He used to wear a long black coat,
>   All buttoned down before."

In his poem "John Gilpin," William Cowper enlists the help of a button to vividly describe a cloak flying away in the wind:

> "The wind did blow, the cloak did fly
> like streamer and gay,
> Till loop and button failing both
> at last it flew away."

Mark Twain in his classic book, *Roughing It,* enhanced the action of a scene with buttons when Horace Greeley made a stage coach trip from New York to California. When Greeley's head crashed through the top of the stage coach, all the buttons were jolted off his coat.

In his amusing book about a boy's life during the early 1900s called *The Chip on Grandma's Shoulder,* Robert Keith Leavitt makes humorous use of buttons when he describes the suits that the grandmother made her two grandsons using cloth and patterns of the 1876 era. "The jackets were long, in an age when store-bought suit coats were short . . . with belts fastened with buttons that could be worn either very tight or very loose but not half way between. And the coats buttoned clear up to the neck . . . The buttons, moreover, were about the diameter of small saucers, and darkly iridescent in hue."

In the poem, "A Hundred Collars," Robert Frost wrote, "He sat there fumbling the buttons on a well-starched shirt."

One of the most memorable descriptive uses of buttons in literature is from *Lassie Come Home* by Eric M. Knight. There was a traveling potter named Rowlie Palmer, who

> "was a little cheery man with a red face that somehow seemed full of buttons. His eyes were like buttons, his weatherbeaten lips were like buttons. There were odd bumps and warts on his forehead and chin that were like buttons. The button similarity went into the actual practice in his clothes. He wore a knitted woolen overshirt which was dotted with pearl shell buttons at every available place. Over that he wore a curious corduroy jacket with leather sleeves, and on that were numerous brass buttons which, if one had inspected further, would have been shown plainly as one-time fasteners of tunics in His Majesty's Army."

Buttons have been devices that writers have used to further the plots of their stories. From *The Highland Widow,* Sir Walter Scott wrote ". . . it was not until he had fired off most of the silver buttons from his waistcoat, and the soldiers, no longer deterred by fear of the unerring marksman . . ."

Buttons were central to the plot of famous Swedish writer August Strindberg's *Island of the Blessed,* published in 1883. In it, children had to collect buttons and classify them as educational therapy. A university was founded, and Buttonology became a compulsory subject.

Laura Ingalls Wilder's books are full of incidents involving buttons that are important to the story lines. In *Little Town on the Prairie,* there is a detailed account of Ma making a button lamp from one of Pa's overcoat buttons from the button bag, a small square of calico, a saucer and axle grease. In *On the Banks of Plum Creek,* there is a lengthy section on the making of a button-string for Carrie's Christmas present. "Ma had saved buttons since she was smaller than Laura, and she had buttons her mother had saved when her mother was a little girl. There were blue buttons and red buttons, silvery and goldy buttons, curved-in buttons with tiny raised castles and bridges and trees on them, and twinkling jet buttons, painted china buttons, striped buttons, buttons like juicy blackberries, and even one tiny dog-head button. Laura squealed when she saw it."

In *The Tale of Peter Rabbit* by Beatrix Potter, Peter got caught by the buttons on his jacket when he tried to escape from Mr. McGregor: ". . . I think he might have got away altogether if he had not unfortunately run into a gooseberry net and got caught by the large buttons on his jacket. It was a blue jacket with brass buttons, quite new."

Bilbo, in *The Hobbit* by J. R. R. Tolkien, had similar button trouble. He got stuck in a door during his escape from goblins because his buttons wedged. When he "gave a terrific squirm," his brass buttons burst, leaving them to be picked up by the goblins.

Dorothy Sayers wrote in *The Unpleasantness at the Bellona Club,* "Felicity calmly informed them one morning that she had gone out before breakfast and actually got married, in the most indecent secrecy and haste, to a middle-aged man called Dormer, very honest and abundantly wealthy, and—horrid to relate—a prosperous manufacturer. Buttons, in fact—made of papier mache or something, with a patent indestructible shank—were the revolting antecedents to which this headstrong Victorian had allied herself."

In *The Man Without a Country,* Edward Everett Hale adeptly used buttons in his plot. Nolan's act of treason was that he declared he never wanted to hear the name of his country again, and his punishment carried out that wish by depriving him of the sight as well as the sound. "They called him 'Plain-Buttons' because, while he always chose to wear the regulation army-uniform, he was not permitted to wear the regulation army-button, for the reason that it bore either the initials or the insignia of the country he had disowned."

One of O. Henry's most famous stories, "A Municipal Report," ended with a button that held the key to the story and told who committed the murder. "I left the city the next morning at nine, and as the train was crossing the bridge over the Cumberland River I took out of my pocket a yellow horn overcoat button the size of a fifty-cent piece, with frayed ends of coarse twine hanging from it, and cast it out of the window into the slow, muddy waters below."

In *Proud New Flags* by F. van Wyck Mason, an historical novel of the Confederate Navy in the years 1861–62, there were several references to the bright buttons on the uniforms. In one case, Semmes used one of his Confederate buttons as a seal on the wax of a letter. The button "depicted a full-rigged ship at sea, surrounded by a circlet of eleven stars within a circle of rope, all in a very pretty design."

Buttons played important parts in the plots of these mysteries written in the mid 1900s: *A Certain Dr. Thorndyk* by R. Austin Freeman, *Button, Button,* a Crime Club book by Marion Bramhall involving a very expensive Louis XIV jeweled button and a murder in a button club in New England, *The Affair of the Sixth Button,* an Armchair Mystery by Clifford Knight and *The Mother Hunt,* a mystery novel by Rex Stout, in which all the most important clues involve rare and unusual buttons.

Another mystery where buttons played a part in the plot is *The Return of Sherlock Holmes* by Ernest Dudley. "They had spent the morning among the ashes of the burned woodpile, and besides the charred remains they had procured several discoloured metal discs. I examined them with care, and there was no doubt that they were trouser buttons. I even distinguished that one of them was marked with the name of 'Hymas,' who was Oldacre's tailor."

In the 1948 book, *Matilda's Buttons,* a girl named Matilda received a present from her mother which was a set of buttons with her family's pictures on them. Matilda formed a friendship with an orphan girl, who came to love Matilda's mother and fondled the "mother" button so much that it fell off Matilda's dress. The button incident resulted in the adoption of the girl by Matilda's mother.

Lewis Carroll set a fantasy scene using imaginary buttons as metaphors in *Alice Through the Looking Glass:*

"He said, 'I hunt for haddocks eyes
Among the heather bright,
And work them into waistcoat buttons
In the silent night'."

Two children's books from the mid-1900s that relied on buttons for plot were *The Charm String* by Bess Torian Palenske and Howard E Wilson, about a girl who is given her grandmother's charm string and *Mr. Pink and the House on the Roof* by Edith Head about the owner of a button factory who kept his factory from becoming a zipper factory.

In a later short story for children called "Big Jack" by Gabrielle E. Jackson, buttons played an instrumental role in the plot. Big Jack was a horse who was fed sugar cubes every day by a young girl. Their ritual was that Big Jack had to nuzzle the buttons on the girl's coat in order to get his sugar lumps—one lump for each of the four buttons. Eventually, the girl moved away. After five years, she revisited Big Jack, who remembered the ritual, but found no buttons to nuzzle on the young ladies' coat because styles had changed! He shook his head and stamped his foot. Of course, he got his sugar lumps anyway.

In a book for older children involving buttons and set during the Revolutionary War called *Buttons for General Washington,* Peter Roop reconstructs a possible mission of a fourteen-year-old spy who carried messages in the buttons of his coat to George Washington's camp.

A children's picture book called *Corduroy* by Don Freeman attached major importance in the story to a missing button on a stuffed bear named Corduroy.

Another picture book, *Bone Button Borscht,* by Aubrey Davis has a fresh version of a familiar folk tale, *Stone Soup.* Instead of using stones for the soup, of course, this version uses buttons. The button soup brings social life back to the community of a miserable European village.

Buttons enhanced the drama in *The Green Years,* a story of life in Scotland around 1900, by A. J. Cronin. "My thin arms flailed the air in wild circular sweeps. I hit Gavin often but always in the hardest and most resistant areas, like his elbows, his cheekbones, and especially the square metal buttons of his kilt. The unfairness of these dreadful buttons move me to a surging bitterness."

Oliver Wendell Holmes moves the action along in his poem, "The Music Grinders," with a scene that involves a button:

> "It cannot be—it is,—it is—
> A hat is going round
> Go very quietly and drop
> A button in the hat."

Robert Frost immortalized the button box in his tale, *In the Witch of Coos.* The old woman in Yankeeland says,

> "Summoning spirits isn't 'Button, button,
> Who's got the button'," I would let them know."

Among the bone buttons the woman saw "finger pieces slid in all directions . . . Where did I see one of those pieces lately? Hand me my button-box. It must be there." At the end of the tale about the haunting ghost, she says:

> "She hadn't found the finger-bone she wanted
> Among the buttons poured out in her lap."

From J. B. Bartlett's *Cry Above the Winds* in the 1830s, a man was shot for the crime of stealing one button. This conversation preceded the shooting: "Anastacio," explained Don Carlos, "has a problem. He is an Indian and Indians do not understand the white man's law. When they see something they want they think themselves fools not to take it. Anastacio stole a gold button—*one* gold button—from a soldier's uniform. He was caught and sentenced to prison. He has already been a year in jail."

In *Life with Father,* Clarence Day has a chapter called "Father Sews on a Button," where buttons provide humor: "Buttons were Father's worst trial, from his point of view. Ripped shirts and socks with holes in them could still be worn but drawers with their buttons off couldn't. The speed with which he dressed seemed to discourage his buttons and make them desert Father's service. Furthermore, they always gave out suddenly and at the wrong time."

Buttons were mentioned several times in the play "L'Aiglon," by Edmond Rostand and were at one point in the story important to the plot. A tailor explained that a waistcoat should have six buttons, but that it was fashionable to leave three of them open. However, each officer's coat had seven buttons.

Button expressions in writing have masterfully communicated characters' opinions on various subjects. In Rabelais' *Works Book I,* a situation was summed up with the phrase, "He did not care a button for it." In *Gargantua and Pantagruel,* the same author told of an action that was not worth more than "l'estimation d'un bouton" (not worth a button.) Edward Lear in *Jumblies* wrote, "But we don't care a button! We don't care a fig!" In "Miss T," Walter de la Mare's character said, "Not a rap, not a button it matters . . ."

Writers have also made fine analogies with buttons. Thomas Hood, the English poet wrote:

"Said Tim unto those jurymen,
   You need not waste your breath,
For I confess myself at once
   The author of her death.
And oh!—when I reflect upon
   The blood that I have spilt,
Just like a button is my soul,
   Inscribed with double guilt!"

This analogy was in *The Master Builder* by Henrik Ibsen: "I am a button moulder, and you must be popped into my casting ladle."

Mark Twain said in *Autobiography* that "Biographies are but the clothes and buttons of the man—the biography of the man himself cannot be written." Many biographers who fell short of their subject would have done well to heed this advice for who can see more than the buttons we put on for public display?

In *A Lifetime with Mark Twain* by Mary Lawton, she quoted, "... he didn't wear shirts buttoned in front like they used to wear in them days. He didn't like those shirts, so he had a man in Hartford make his shirts special for him with the buttons on the back..."

In *Jonathan Fisher,* Mary Ellen Chase told of a man who was a minister and a jack-of-all trades during 1772–1847. The button industry was mentioned in the diary entries of nearly every year. "Literally nothing which could be turned into monetary gain was wasted or overlooked. The bones of slaughtered farm animals were kept and made into thousands of buttons, filed and pierced by the entire family, sometimes dyed in various colors and sold at twenty-five cents a dozen." One diary entry stated, "One dozen buttons in return for two pounds of cheese."

Lord Byron wrote in his diary on December 7, 1813: "Awoke and up an hour before being called: but dawdled three hours in dressing. When we subtract from life, infancy (which is vegetation)—sleeping, eating and swilling—buttoning and unbuttoning—how much remains of downright existence?"

In *Goebbels' Diary* in 1942, Joseph Goebbels, the Nazi propagandist, wrote of General MacArthur, "You don't get to be a great general by letting pedestrians wear your picture in their buttonholes."

Elinor Graham records the positive effect she perceived buttons to have on a community in her *Maine Charm String*. She wrote, "It was through buttons that I discovered the uniquely generous quality of my neighbors. While looking at buttons, we could exchange ideas. Buttons were the touchstone. They freed tongues."

Gertrude Stein, in *Everybody's Autobiography* wrote,

"We were going to America . . . Of course I had many new shoes, I am very fond of new shoes, I do not care a great deal for new clothes, I let them hang a long time before I can wear them but I do like new shoes and at Chambery they made me a great many of them. I was wearing one of them and as I stepped up on the train the button snapped off. Oh Trac, I said. He said wait a minute and off he went and he came back with a button and a needle and a thread and he sewed the button on there, we were once more ready to go away."

Novels in the 1990s use buttons extensively in all the ways of past works. In fact, it's difficult to read a modern novel that doesn't make use of buttons in some way. In *Beach Music* by Pat Conroy, buttons are used heroically to aid in the escape of a young Jewish woman from the Nazis in Poland. "And so Moshe gave her the sixteen gold coins that he kept in a special book . . . And she takes the coins and covers them with cloth, and turns them into buttons, eight for my new dress and eight for my sister's."

Buttons are used not only to further action in books, but to describe obesity, overheating, nervousness, contemplation, sloppiness, neatness, shyness, poverty and drunkenness. One of the most intriguing button uses in modoern literature is in Douglas Kennedy's *Cold Mountain*. One of his twelve mentions of buttons describes a collar button festering out of a Civil War wound in the main character.

Buttons enhance the graphic sexuality found in literature nowadays. In *Sabboth's Theater,* Philip Roth makes nine sexually related button reference, such as "The speed with which Drenka unbuttoned Christa's jacket and with which Christa undid Dranka's silk blouse and cleared aside her push-up bra astonished Sabbath."

John Irving, in *A Widow for One Year,* also uses buttons amorously: "She had left the buttons unbuttoned and the long sleeves of the sweater pulled back, as if an invisible woman in the cardigan had clasped her invisible hands behind her invisible head."

Writers in the past, if not as explicit as contemporary writers, found efffective ways to convey perversities of life through buttons. In *The Total Depravity of Inanimate Things* in 1864, Katherine Kent Child Walker wrote, "The elusiveness of soap, the knottiness of strings, the transitory nature of buttons . . ."

Fitzhugh Ludlow in the 1800s told his readers:

"While we wait for the napkin, the soup gets cold,
While the bonnet is trimming, the face grows old,
When we've matched our buttons, the pattern is sold
And everything comes too late—too late."

William James wrote in *Essays in Radical Empiricism,* "'The through-and-through universe seems to suffocate me with its infallible impeccable all pervasiveness . . . It seems too buttoned up and white-chokered and clean-shaven a thing . . ."

The Reverend Laurence Sterne in *Tristram Shandy* asked, "What is life of man? Is it not to shift from side to side, from sorrow to sorrow? To button up one cause of vexation and unbutton another?"

On a more positive side, Benjamin Franklin wrote:

"Do'st thou love life?
Then do not waste or squander time,

for that is the stuff life is made of . . .
Let us all say . . .
    There's time for kindness
    And for giving.
    Time for buttoning
    And Happy Living."

Button Talk
(Button Expressions)

The world of buttons has its own language, especially regarding the competitive judging of button trays at shows. Words like goofies, ringers, igloos and measles abound. (See definition box on this page.)

In a St. Louis hotel where a button convention was being held, several button collectors were once talking in an elevator about the judging of their tray of heads (buttons showing heads of people), when a man asked if they were a group of morticians. He could just as easily heard them say how much they really like studs or their collections of rubbers.

There are specialized button expressions that button collectors sometimes use. "Going on a button bender or a button binge" means a button shopping spree.

"Button biographies" refers to the individual history behind each button.

"An attack of button measles" means in the United States National Button Society that a person has made many mistakes on the trays for competition at a button show. It also sometimes means that a person is wearing many buttons.

Goofies are buttons that are realistic in form.
Ringers and igloos are types of china buttons.
Measles is a term used to describe a mistake made on competitive button card at button shows.
Studs are buttons that appear on both sides of material with the primary button on the front and an attachment on the back.
Rubbers are buttons made of vulcanized rubber.

"Button Addict," "buttonaire," "button bug," "buttonist," "buttonite," "buttonophile" and "fibulatist" (which is derived from the Latin word meaning fastener) all refer to button collectors.

"A button buddy" means a fellow button collector.

"Buttonic news" means something new in the way of buttons.

"Smothered" refers to the technique used by the London Pealies to sew on buttons to their costumes in such a way that the fabric can't be seen due to the quantity of buttons.

A "poke box" is a box or other container full of inexpensive, assorted buttons that collectors poke through and scoop out, often at button shows, looking for bargains. Collectors consider this activity great fun.

Buttons have been responsible for symbolic phrases used in everyday speech. For instance, the phrase "He's lost his buttons" or "She has a few buttons missing" has come to mean the person has lost some brain power or sanity. Buttons, like the brain, hold us together.

One origination of the phrase came from the 1600s when the well-dressed man was judged by the number and beauty of the buttons on his coat. They were made of precious metals and jewels. Often the dandies were attacked by thugs who stole the buttons, after slugging them so hard they would stagger around in a stupor. People asked, "Have you lost your buttons?"

Another source for the phrase comes from the Orient, where buttons on the cap indicated the studies a scholar had completed. If he hadn't yet achieved honors or had failed in the pursuit of knowledge, it was said, "He hasn't all his buttons."

There are military expressions with button connotations:
"Pat as a doughboy" means suitable or fitting ("doughboy" refers to the uniform buttons of the United States Infantry in the Civil War and later to the Infantry soldiers themselves and again to American soldiers in World War I).

"Button chopper" means a laundry.

"Button up" means to close up a tank, used in armored units.

"Tank unbuttoned" means a tank with its hatch and slips open.

"Buttoned up" is an English term meaning "all prepared." It is seldom used in the United States, but when used, means that orders have been carried out.

The phrase, "Not worth a button," was in use as early as the fourteenth century. The earliest reference to buttons in the Oxford English Dictionary is dated 1320 and relates to this phrase. It was an indication that comparatively cheap buttons were being used at that time for all but the wealthy or noble.

"Bubbling" is an expression that appears in documents and history from the 1600s and 1700s. It refers to the slashing off of a theft victim's buttons.

The English expression, "As worthless as a Brummagem Button," means that something is shoddy. The phrase originated because the button manufacturers of Birmingham, England, so reduced the thin coatings of gold put on brass buttons that three pennies' worth of gold was made to cover a whole gross of buttons. This scanty use of gold brought forth the odious comparison.

"Bright as a button," means smart. The expression came from the Golden Age of Buttons and was originally "Bright as a Birmingham button."

"Cute as a button" originated in 1946 according to *Listening to America* in 1982 by Stuart Berg Flexner.

The phrase "neat as a button" is listed under synonyms for the adjective "clean" in *Roget's 21st Century Thesaurus*. "Button down" is listed under "consummate" in the same source.

"Button man" is an American slang term for a rank and file member of the Mafia.

"Don't bust your buttons," is what people in Australia say when someone is getting upset.

"On the button" is a boxing expression referring to the point of the chin.

There are other common expressions rooted in buttons:
"Pardon me while I pop my buttons a little," means to brag.
"There's more to this button than meets the buttonhole," means there's something else going on that isn't immediately evident.
"Right on the button," means something is correct or perfect.
"Button up!" is a way to tell someone to be quiet.
"Dash my button!" is an old-fashioned expletive.
To be "buttonholed" by someone means to be held in conversation with the person in such a way that it would be impolite to leave.

"Taken down a buttonhole" refers to a person who is too clever for his own good.

"He has more buttons than holes," means something or someone doesn't quite make sense.

"Button up your overcoat" is an expression that conveys warmth and regard.

"Migrating buttons" refers to buttons that are moved from one article of clothing to another.

The expression "brass buttons" suggests authority and service.

"Buttonscapes" are pictures "painted" with buttons. This used to be a very popular type of art from the 1940s to 1960s.

"Push button" refers to a modern approach to life, to speed and efficiency.

The term "happy button" has been used to describe a woman's clitoris.

A "buttoned-down" person, group or affair would be very conservative.

Button phrases have long been used, along with real buttons, on greeting cards. Some of the messages have been: "I love you from the *button* of my heart," "Your news is *fastenating*," "I have *buttons* in my eyes for you," "Am I *buttin'* in?" "Just *buttin'* in to wish you a happy or merry . . ." and "I'm *attached* to you."

A stud is a button which appears on both sides of the material through which it is put, with the primary button on the front and an attachment on the back.

Strap buttons not larger than three-fourths inch were used for suspenders. The same kind, when larger than that, were called "bangup buttons. "

In the Old South, the slaves skewered their "galluses" to their pants with wooden pins or thorns of the locust. Such fastenings were called "Georgia buttons."

Bachelor buttons were simple devises made in the late 1800s to avoid the bother of having to find a needle and thread to sew on a button, or the struggle of forcing a stud through the thickness of material. By means of a removable back-stud, they could be attached in an instant. In 1941 they advertised, "No thread, no needle, no sewing—for men and boys."

During their early manufacture in 1870–1890, bachelor buttons were called solitaires.

Spinster buttons also existed. These were made in a brooch-like way, for example a butterfly which clipped onto a back-stud. The stud had a very sharp point, but it snapped on in the same way as a bachelor button.

Padlock buttons were probably a type of Bachelor button. The directions said: "Place lock over head of shank and force to center."

The Buttoneer was an instant button attacher that was placed on the market in 1968. It did not require a needle and thread. This invention attached one-hole buttons, which came with the kits, as well as standard set-through and shanked buttons.

The noun "button" did not become a verb until the thirteenth century.

Webster's New Encyclopedic Dictionary defines a button as, "a small knob or disc used for holding parts of a garment together or as an ornament."

Webster, in his 1852 dictionary, says the word "button" is from French "bouton" meaning a bud. Botwm is Welsh, bottum is Cornish, bottoni is Italian, boton is Spanish, belgic is Dutch, bot is Armenian and boton is Portugese. All are from the root of "bud."

Funny Buttons
(Button Jokes and Quotes)

To become a subject for jokes, something must usually enter frequently into our lives. It's no wonder then that buttons have been the brunt of buffoonery for hundreds of years.

In the 1700s when buttons were big and bold, they were often the subjects of caricature-type cartoons. One such cartoon featured a man whose buttons were ridiculously exaggerated to larger than normal size. Another, captioned "Coup de Bouton," showed a man greeting a woman, and the effect of the brilliant, huge and numerous buttons on his coat gave the woman a "sunstroke."

In 1719, a comedy called "LaMode," played at an Italian playhouse. It was about the discovery of a secret which permitted making buttons so infinitesimal "that one was not able to button his own clothes except with a microscope."

In 1764, after Parliament had issued many restrictive regulations on manufacturing and commerce in the colonies, Benjamin Franklin wrote a caustic letter containing button humor to Peter Collison in England. It said,

> "... we have discovered a beach in a bay several miles round, the pebbles of which are all in the form of buttons, whence it is called Buttonmould Bay; where thousands of tons may be had for fetching; and as the sea washes down the slay cliff, more are continually manufacturing out of the fragments by the surge. I send you a specimen of coat, waistcoat and sleeve buttons; just as nature has turned them. But I think I must not mention the place, lest some Englishman get a patent for this button-mine, as one did for the coal mine at Louisburgh ..."

Button jokes have been recorded from as early as the turn of the twentieth century:

    A teacher was trying to show a small boy how to read with expression.

    "Where are you going?" read Johnny, in a laborious monotone.

    "Try that again," said the teacher. "But read as if you were talking. Don't you see that mark at the end?"

    Johnny studied the interrogation point. Suddenly an idea dawned on him. He read triumphantly, "Where are you going, little buttonhook?"

Students have used buttons in the classroom too, as Susie did when her teacher asked who could make a sentence using fascinate. Susie's answer was, "My coat has ten buttons, but I can fasten only eight.

Buttons have often been involved in humorous domestic situations. In 1869, *Godey's Lady's Book* said the new invention of the corkscrew button, which didn't have to be sewn, was an invention that would enable men to keep the buttons on their shirts and to do away with wives altogether.

    A cartoon caption from an old newspaper showed a woman saying, "If those button-down-the-back dresses get popular again, we're going to need a husband or a long buttonhook."

    In 1962, the *National Button Bulletin* facetiously reported that "the real cause of the fall in the marriage market is the substitution of studs and bolted buttons for the mother-of-pearl and thread kinds."

    A long-standing marital conflict revolves around sewing on buttons. The Broadway musical, "Grounds for Divorce" based on a play written in 1851, featured a comic duet brought about by the wife forgetting to sew a button on her husband's shirt.

    "Old Soloman had a thousand wives. He probably kept trying until he found one who would sew on a button," was a quote by Robert Quillen.

    There is a story about a husband who showed his wife a photograph of himself. "Why, she exclaimed, "two of your coat buttons are off!"

    "I'm glad you finally noticed," he said. "That's the reason I had the picture taken."

    There's another similar joke: "This is news," said the wife. "Someone has invented a shirt without buttons."

    "There's nothing new about that," said the husband. "I've been wearing them that way ever since I became a button collector's husband."

    A 1940s toast from a man was, "Here's to my wife, the lady who is expected to buy without funds and to sew on buttons before they come off."

    An unknown author has summed up the marital button situation appropriately with this statement:

"A darn important question asked ever and anon
Is not 'Who's got the button,' but 'Who will sew it on'."

Church button jokes have been around for decades. It is said that putting buttons in the collection plates during the Depression was common. One cartoon proclaimed: "Notice in a Scottish Church—those who prefer to put buttons rather than money in the offertory are asked to put in their own buttons, not those from the cushions."

Jokes like the following ones also come as a result of church tithing practices:

"Daddy," said the little girl at the Sunday dinner table, "didn't the minister say this morning that the heathens don't wear clothes?"

"Yes, my daughter," said the father.

"Then why did you put a button in the missionary collection?' asked the daughter.

"Do you think times are getting better," asked the church visitor.

"Oh yes, decidedly," said the Pastor. "We are getting a much better class of buttons in the collection plate now."

A British cartoon depicts a bum at the door of a house, and a housewife who is answering the door. He says, as he hands her a button, "You look to be a good Christian lady. Would you sew a shirt on this button?"

Question: Why does a Russian soldier wear brass buttons on his coat and a German wear steel buttons?

Answer: To keep their coats buttoned.

A nanny said, "Say young man, how do you expect me to sew on this suspender button if you keep wiggling around like that?"

The nanny gave the boy a cookie to eat to keep him still.

"Works like a charm," said the nanny. "I'll have to remember this."

"Oops, looks like the button came off the other side too!" said the boy.

Little Marvin found a button in his salad. He remarked, "I suppose it fell off while the salad was dressing."

What goes around a but-ton? A billy goat.

A trade journal in the 1950s, referring to specialization printed the following:

"Button! Button! This we are told, is the age of specialization. Just find yourself needing a little medical attention and, brother, you will discover just how right they are! An anxious mother telephoned a physician and begged, "Come quickly, doctor! My little August has swallowed a button!"

"A button?" the medic rejoined, as cool as a cucumber. "What kind of a button?"

"Celluloid," the mother replied. "It came from—"

"I'm sorry," the doctor interrupted, "but you'll have to call Dr. Adamson if its celluloid. I remove only metal ones with an embossed design."

During a pause around the bridge table, one of the ladies asked the hostess, "I suppose you carry some sort of memento in your locket-button?"

"Yes," she replied, "It's a lock of my husband's hair."

"But your husband is still alive!"

"Yes, of course," said the hostess.

"But his hair is gone."

Bill—"Have you heard our suspender-button song?"
Pete—"No, what's its name?"
Bill—"It All Depends on You."

Buttons themselves have brought laughter from many a spectator because of their strategic placements and innuendoes. The Flapper buttons decorating women's garters in the 1920s sometimes featured a policeman with his hand held up in the "stop" position. In the 1960s, there were suggestive sweater buttons for women depicting street signs in the appropriate shapes: STOP, SOFT SHOULDERS, CURVES AHEAD, DANGER, PROCEED WITH CAUTION, SLOWDOWN and DEAD END. The implications haven't always been directed toward women, however. A woman in England has a button from a man's fly inscribed "gentlemen only."

In addition to making us laugh, buttons have been symbols from which we've made analogies. One is, "People are like buttons, always popping off at the wrong time." Another from *Sunshine Magazine* is "People are like buttonholes, since their value is not apparent until they become attached to something important, and then they often prove themselves valuable to the world."

A number of well-known people have "button talked" or been "button talked about." One of the earliest was Goethe, who said, "If you miss the first buttonhole, you will not succeed in buttoning up your coat."

"I had a soul above buttons," said George Coleman, Jr., the English dramatist.

An observer of General Winfield Scott, United States presidential candidate in 1852, once described the grumpy-looking man as having a "mouth that could be covered with a button."

From outer space an astronaut told us, "Earth looks like a beautiful blue and white button laid on black velvet."

Sidney Joseph Perelman, according to Bartlett's Familiar Quotations, described himself as being, "Button-cute, rapier-keen, wafer-thin and pauper poor."

In 1953, Hedda Hopper, the Hollywood columnist, asserted that woman's independence from her husband began when she stopped wearing dresses with twenty-four buttons down the back!"

"I've always considered a fallen button as God's way of telling us the shirt was wrong," came from Erma Bombeck.

"As you travel through life my friend, keep your eye upon the button and not upon the hole," came from Sandra Foster, past President of the Australian Button Collectors Society.

Wise or clever button sayings also have come from unknown people:
"If you don't want to sew on a button, sew the buttonhole shut."
"Buttons are things with which people are all familiar but know nothing about."
"It's a lot easier to get Grandpa's whiskers out of a button than it is a zipper."
"A fellow who sits around wondering why the buttonholes in his shirt are vertical while those in his coat are horizontal, isn't earning whatever he's being paid."

There have been amusing real-life button stories with comical twists. In 1890 when Lord Salisbury traded the little island of Heligoland in the North Sea to Germany for territory in Africa and the island of Zanzibar, he said, "We have traded the pant buttons for a pair of pants."

In the 1920s when men's pants had buttons rather than zippers, sometimes the buttons came unbuttoned. In mixed company on these occasions, a guy would say to the one unbuttoned, "It's one o'clock in the button factory."

The late Monica Jones in England used to put buttons she didn't like together on a card which she called her "Ugly Card," until a friend pointed out that she'd given Monica one of the buttons on it. "Mind you," Monica said, "I still think it's awful!"

Doormen at the Holiday Inn in Edinburgh, Scotland, wear kilt-style uniforms that are decorated extensively with buttons. One doorman said the ten buttons by the back pleat of the jacket were there to cover up the holes his wife made when she threw darts at him.

A knitter said that she spent six weeks knitting a sweater and another six weeks finding the right buttons for it.

A mother was mailing her son the overcoat he forgot to take to college, and she wrote: "Dear Son, Your coat is so heavy I cut off the buttons to save postage. Love and kisses, Mom. P. S. The buttons are in the right-hand pocket."

There was a little girl playing with her grandma's button box who took a glass flecked button to Grandma and said, "See the button with freckles on it!"

Another small girl who was learning to dress herself came tearfully to her mother with the question, "How can I button my dress when the buttons are on the back, and I'm on the front?"

It was said of William Rollinson, the man who made buttons worn by George Washington at the first Inauguration, that in his youth he was brought up to be a "chaser of fine buttons." (Chasing was a type of metal work.) This term properly describes button collectors, although their chasing is different from that practiced by Rollinson.

Did You Know?
(Fascinating Button Bits)

King Louis IX of France is credited with linking two buttons together to create the cuff link in the 1200s.

The earliest reference to buttons quoted in the *Compact Oxford English Dictionary* was from "Sir Gawain and the Grene Knight," a poem in 1340: "On botounz of ye bryzt grene brayden ful ryche." (On buttons made of bright rich fabric.)

Mary, Queen of Scots, wore jet and pearl acorn buttons to her execution in 1587.

From the 1200s, wills record fathers leaving sets of buttons to their sons along with titles and social status. It was common for kings in England and France through the 1800s to mention their buttons in their wills. In George III's will, he left forty coat buttons worth 4,000 pounds sterling and twenty-six waistcoat buttons worth 1,000 pounds sterling.

Button handkerchiefs also were left to relatives in wills. The will of Mary Ring, who died in 1631, left her son Andrew "all her handkerchiefs, buttoned or unbuttoned."

Frogs (braidings for fastening a garment that consist of a button and a loop through which they pass) have been called Brandenburgs after the town in Germany where they were used on military uniforms in the late 1600s.

In the 1700s, French encyclopedist Denis Diderot devoted eight pages to buttons and button makers.

Prior to 1750, gold and silver buttons were just that. In 1742 in England, the plating process was invented. Dandies bought plated buttons by the gross because they could not be differentiated from solid gold unless one looked underneath at the copper foundation. And that wasn't polite, at least not in public. After 1840, the electroplating process was invented.

Buttons in factories used to be counted using a paddle-like board which had 144 holes. The worker would dip this device down into a barrel of buttons, and it would come up well covered with them. The worker gave the board an experienced shake, and each hole would have only one button.

Buttons with various types of attachment gimmicks have periodically been manufactured. To facilitate laundering, buttons used to be supplied with clips that went through the eyelets in the garment and were secured with the clips. The buttons could then be easily removed.

There were buttons made with detachable shanks that were patented in 1842.

In *Godey's Ladies Book* in 1867, a new kind of button was listed—one which fastened on cloth without thread. It had a small corkscrew effect in wire on the back instead of a shank. It pressed into the cloth and formed a ring that held the button in place.

There have been buttons made with one hole on the top and two holes drilled into the bottom which don't show on the front. Button collectors call them "whistle" buttons.

There was another type of one-holed button made in the 1700s by the Wedgewood firm. The button was attached by guiding the thread up a hole through a separate gold bead on the top and back down through the same hole.

Snap buttons were once advertised in a catalog "for the use of the traveling man, the farmer, the laborer, the mechanic, the growing boy and his father of every profession, . . . can instantly replace his missing buttons."

In 1909, George Jervis designed a line of postal cards featuring people with painted panty-waist real buttons for faces. They were referred to as the "Button Family Postcards."

Avon introduced a four-hole button soap in the 1970s, and about the same time Hallmark made wrapping paper with beautiful buttons on it.

In 1971, iron-on buttons hit the market. Shirt-type buttons came presewed to iron-on patches. They were advertised to withstand thirty trips through the washer and dryer.

In 1981, Arlene Altman of Los Angeles created copies of the small, four-hole bone buttons sewn to button-down collar shirts by Brooks Brothers. However, these differed in two ways. First, they didn't sew on. Instead, they were easily detachable and could be moved from one shirt to another. Second, her buttons cost $110 a pair because they were made out of fourteen-carat gold.

Buttons can be sewn on a fabric strip or tape and used for temporary buttons on a garment by wearing the strip under the garment. In Elizabethan time, strips of leather were used for this purpose.

The backs of buttons are frequently very beautifully and interestingly made and are sometimes ornamental. There are functional uses for button backs as well. Buttons' pedigrees are often more clearly read on the back than the face. Registry marks, swirl marks, and backmarks often bear the record of the button's own history—factory names, political sayings, words and ornamental designs. Quality marks such as "superb quality," "extra rich superfine," "non plus ultra," exist. Location marks, advertising marks and gimmicks are on button backs. The button makers of the early 1800s seemed to hold entirely blank backs in complete contempt. Tailors were allowed to have their names stamped on the backs of buttons if the firm ordered

(back)

U.S. General Staff Officer coat button

(front)

(back)

Joan of Arc button

large quantities from the manufacturer. Backmarks on buttons were used as early as the 1600s to tell purchasers who the makers were.

It is also true that backmarks have been extensively used to deceive the customer about where the button was made. During the last half of the 1800s, the French button makers had world-wide prestige for button designs and finishes, so button makers from other countries tried to disguise their buttons as French by backmarking them with french phrases like "La Mode Parisienne" or "Ne plus ultra."

Catgut shanks on buttons have no relationship to cats. The catgut string laced through molds from the 1700s came from goats and sheep.

Buttonholes historically have been a matter of ornament as well as of use. For one of her birthdays, Princess Anna at English Court was given an azure velvet coat for her son, the little Duke of Gloucester. The buttonholes were encrusted with diamonds.

In 1685, King Louis XIV of France had a jacket made with forty-eight buttons of gold, each with a diamond and ninety-six buttonholes of which forty-eight contained five diamonds each and forty-eight had a single diamond each, worth 185,123 livres.

Buttonholes were carefully cut and bound in bright colors, embroidered with silver and gold thread and bound with vellum. In old-time letters there are directions about modish button holes and drawings, too. This advertisement ran in the *New England Weekly Journal* in 1737: "Silver and Gold Thread for Button Holes and Silver and Gold Sleazy Thread for Stitching and Embroidering."

Although button covers have become a popular fad, they have been around for centuries. Long ago they were made of black velvet and worn by gentlemen over fashionable brass buttons when the brass lost its shine. They were worn to funerals and church services, and they were called button caps.

There have been several patents taken out for shoe button covers which used to be popular. The little gadgets dressed up shoes by slipping over the strap, then over the shoe button.

Long, strong buttonhooks were used in the past for buttoning boots and gaiters. Medium-sized button hooks were used for outdoor gloves and small and dainty hooks were used for delicate gloves and carried in evening bags. The inventor of shoe laces became a millionaire when he found a better method than buttons for fastening shoes.

Did You Know?

The word "blazer" is derived from an old English ship, the Blazer. The captain decided to spruce up his crew by having them wear solid, blue jackets with metal buttons. These became known as blazers. Today they are patterned as well as plain, but a true blazer is always metal-buttoned.

Satsuma buttons come from Satsuma, Japan, but weren't originally made by the Japanese. When the Japanese invaded Korea, they took people back in bondage to Satsuma, and the slaves made the buttons.

Buttons were the first product in the United States' commercial history to be advertised continentally. The pioneer national advertiser was Caspar Wistar, who began manufacturing and publicizing what he called "Philadelphia Brass Buttons" in the 1720s.

The earliest American advertisement specifically for buttons was in 1838 in the *Missouri Republican*. The buttons advertised included ones made of "bone, pearl, gilt and "lasting" mohair and silk."

The Industrial Exhibition of 1851 was inspired by Prince Albert as a result of an inspection of Birmingham's button industry.

Professor J. K. Galbraith, the pioneer of time-work studies, experimented to see if it was quicker to button a waistcoat up or down. He found that time was saved if one started at the bottom. He is also credited with estimating that prior to general use of zipper fasteners, an average man did up 11,200 buttons per year.

Buttons have often been subjects of superstition. According to *The Button Lovers Book* by Marilyn Green, superstitions have grown from the use of buttons. One is that attaching a white button with black thread or a black button with white thread will make the seamstress unpopular. Another has to do with the number of buttons on a wedding dress. If the dress has one or five buttons, the groom will be rich, two or six buttons and he'll be poor, three or seven buttons and he'll be a beggar.

Joyce Whittemore says in *The Book of Buttons* that gypsies believe that buttons are lucky.

Raphael's Book of Dreams from the 1800s says, "If you dream of bright buttons it is good, if rusty, it denotes misfortune, if covered, sadness and sorrow. If a man dreams he has lost buttons off his clothes, it denotes that he will not live long, and will lose money in his business."

In Bohemia, people hold a button on their clothing to bring good luck when they meet a chimney sweep on the street.

In some primitive societies, buttons are worn to ward off evil.

In Sunnyvale, California, a young bride-to-be named Catherine Wire spent months sewing her wedding dress only to find that she had sewed the loops so close to the seam that the forty-three fabric covered buttons wouldn't fit. She checked an old tin of her grandmother's buttons and found exactly forty-three antique mother-of-pearl buttons which fit the loops.

Fear of buttons is a phobia called koumphiphobia. Psychotherapists say it is a rare phobia that can be cured by using hypnotism to reveal the original anxiety.

An old tradition among Moslems and Jews was to use a four-hole button but never to stitch a cross. They felt that the cross was a Christian symbol, so they stitched their buttons in such a way that threads never crossed other threads.

Of all buttons ever made, it is estimated that ninety-nine percent of buttons are round.

In earlier days in Denmark, only married women were allowed to wear silver buttons.

Double-breasted suits have been popular in part because when one front side gets dirty, the jacket can be buttoned up the other side.

There are 126 ways to sew on a four-hole button. There are basic hints that apply to all ways, however. When beginning to sew on a button, place the knot in the thread on the outside of the fabric under the button or between the outside and facing.

Buttons without shanks should be sewn on quite loosely. After a few threads have been passed through the buttons, the thread should be wound several times around those threads between the button and the fabric to make a thread shank. If such a button is sewn very closely to a garment, it won't have room to rest easily in the buttonhole and will make the spacing seem imperfect. The loose sewing and winding also increases the durability.

Three-hole buttons provide a stronger hold to material than two-hole ones because the thread punctures the fabric in three different locations and prevents puncturing the same horizontal or vertical line. Thus the stitching doesn't break the fabric that holds the button, eliminating one of the main reasons that buttons come off.

To cut off buttons from a garment without damaging the garment, hold a comb under the button and use a razor.

The English measure of button size is the line. The French measure is the ligne. They look and sound much alike. However, one does not equal the other. There are forty lines and but only twelve lignes to an inch.

Buttons as small as the size of a pin head and as large as six inches across have been worn.
    The button with the reputation for being the biggest in the world was made for the Williston Academy in Easthampton, Massachusetts, in 1923 as a trophy to grace the table of the class with the largest attendance at the annual dinners of the Williston Alumni of New York. The button is ten inches in diameter and is covered with the school colors of blue and gold. The Williston Academy had been "founded on a button," as related in the chapter, *All Because of a Button*.

The National Button Society classifies buttons in two categories: modern and old, with the dividing line being 1918 because with World War I came drastic changes in button manufacturing. In 1919, there were 557 button manufacturers in the United States, and by 1929 there were less than 200.

When Elinor Graham wrote a book on button collecting in 1946, she proposed the title, *Buttons for My Undoing*, but the publisher would not allow it, citing overtones of pornography! It was published with the title, *Maine Charm String*.

After the Second World War, a man named Emanuel Ress made a supply of buttons with skulls and the following words on them: DEATH—is SO *PERMANENT!* DRIVE CAREFULLY! He submitted the design to the National Safety Council in Chicago with the idea that these buttons should be given out with drivers' licenses. He was informed, however, that "death" was a tabooed word and too morbid also. Ress was stuck with his supply of buttons.

In the 1940s at the Pennsylvania Hotel in New York and the Statler Hotel in Washington, D. C., an array of different buttons sewn on pin cushions was provided for use by the guests.

In 1952, Oregon Representative Walter Norblad announced that every time the Army outfitted itself with a new pair of pants, it wasted twelve million buttons.

The biggest button robbery in the world was in Manila in the 1950s when three armed men held up a warehouse and stole 576,000 military buttons that were packed for delivery to the Philippine Army.

In the 1960s, there was a "button bank" at H. Huntsmans' Sons in London where members of hunt clubs could replace lost buttons for their hunting costumes just by writing and requesting them.

In 1970, a story about buttons and computers appeared in the financial section of an Iowa newspaper. A computer was keeping tabs on the 400 million buttons that the Lansing Company distributed that year. The purpose was to help spot fashion trends in button styles.

In 1977, *Esquire* magazine predicted, "A number of new developments are foreseen in textiles: suits that change color with the press of a button."

In 1981, Random House published two button books for children that were recalled because the Consumer Product Safety Commission declared them unsafe. *My Button Book* and *Hello Kitty's Button Book* both contained real buttons which might have caused a child to choke.

Did You Know?

In 1991, $2,200 was spent at an auction for a button worn at the inauguration of President George Washington. Today, auction prices for campaign buttons that are "graphic beauties" have soared above $10,000.

The designer Norma Kamali has buttons embossed with the name "Ernie" on her denim clothes. Ernie is the name of her dog.

Rhode Island, the nation's smallest state, has the shortest motto on their state buttons—"Hope."

It is said that a beautiful dimple may be acquired by sleeping for a certain number of nights on a collar button.

Enemies to the fancy button are: four holes, modern synthetics, spin dryers, costume jewelry and zippers.

In times past, one could tell a person's good taste and wealth by the kind of buttons he wore on his waistcoat. It's not that easy anymore. A zipper doesn't tell anything about a person.

Buttons are said to have kept their noisy nemesis, the zipper, off the market for thirty years after it was invented.

Of course, buttons don't really compete with zippers. A zipper isn't beautiful. It's strictly utilitarian. A button provides eye appeal. And whoever heard of a family zipper box?

The common button has remained virtually unchanged, irreplaceable and as universal and permanent as the wheel.

Buttons that can be snapped, screwed or tied into place don't stay in fashion. Sticky-tape enclosures prove ineffective. Even zippers have to be secured with a hook or button.

Buttons that button are here to stay.

Bibliography

d'Allemagne, Henry René. *Les Accessoires du Costume et du Mobilier.* Paris: Schemit, 1928.

Boatner, Mark May. *Military Customs and Traditions.* New York: D. McKay Company, 1956.

Boileau, Étienne. *The Book of Trades.* Paris: Imprimerie Nationale, 1879.

Cusick, Dawn. *The Button Craft Book.* New York: Sterling Publishing, 1995.

Emilio, Luis Fenollosa. *The Emilio Collection of Military Buttons.* Salem, MA: (self-published), 1942.

Epstein, Diana. *The Button Book.* Philadelphia: Running Press, 1996.

Epstein, Diana, and Millicent Safro. *Buttons.* New York: Harry N. Abrams, 1991.

Flexner, Stuart Berg. *Listening to America.* New York: Simon & Schuster, 1982.

Forbes, Esther. *Paul Revere and the World He Lived In.* Boston: Houghton Mifflin, 1942.

Graham, Elinor. *Maine Charm String.* New York: Macmillan, 1946.

Green, Marilyn. *The Button Lover's Book.* Radnor, PA: Chilton Book Co., 1991.

Hughes, Elizabeth, and Marion Lester. *The Big Book of Buttons.* Sedgwick, ME: New Leaf Publishers, 1981.

Longford, J. A. *A Century of Birmingham Life.* Birmingham: W. G. Moore & Co., 1870–71.

Luscomb, Sally. *The Collector's Encyclopedia of Buttons.* New York: Crown, 1967; reprinted by Schiffer Publishing Ltd., Atglen, PA, 1993.

Morley, Frank Vigor. *The Great North Road: A Journey in History.* New York: Macmillan, 1961.

Mozart, Wolfgang Amadeus. *Letters of Mozart and His Family.* London: Macmillan, 1985.

Newberger, Edward Louis. *The Button Industry in the United States.* Haworth, NJ: St. Johann Press, 1998.

Osborne, Peggy Ann. *About Buttons: A Collector's Guide – 150 A.D. to the Present.* Atglen, PA: Schiffer Publishing, Ltd., 1994.

Raverat, Gwendolen. *Period Piece*. New York: Norton, 1953.

Roberts, Catherine. *Who's Got the Button*. New York: David McKay Co., 1962.

Smith, Robert C. *Raphael's Book of Dreams* (also titled: *The Book of Dreams: Being a Concise Interpretation of Dreams*). London: W. Foulsham & Co., 1886.

Squire, Gwen. *Buttons*. London: Frederick Muller, 1972.

Whittemore, Joyce. *The Book of Buttons*. New York: Dorling Kindersley, 1992.

Wolff, Edward. *Why We Do It*. New York: Macaulay, 1929.

Young, George Frederick. *The Medici*. London: J. Murray, 1909.

Index

Al Hattab, 11
Alemite buttons, 25
Antiquewear (shop), 1, 109

Benitez, Salvador, 38
Bicycle leggin' buttons, 49
Borgia Family, 13
Braces (suspender) buttons, 4
Bridal buttons, 75, 152
Button gardens, 44, 50–51
Button Museum, 105
Button plague, 5, 71
Button Queen (shop person), 7, 149
Button Store, 34, 117
Byron, Lord George, 24, 175

Camera buttons, 16, 75
Campaign buttons, 22–23, 154
Carrickfergus, Battle of, 18, 135
Cellini, Benvenuto, 66, 112, 140
Charles I (King of England), 36, 56
Charles II (King of England), 36, 88, 159
Civil War, 14, 132, 135, 153, 179
Clark, George Rogers, 57
Compass buttons, 15, 136

Dickens, Charles, 27, 31, 115, 157, 166–168
Dior, Christian, 124
Dorset button industry, 59–60, 161
Duttons for Buttons (shop), 149

Edward I (King of England), 139
Edward III (King of England), 91
Electric sleeve buttons, 154
Elevator buttons, 48

Elizabeth I (Queen of England), 36, 84, 92, 141
Elizabeth II (Queen of England), 93, 145
Emergency buttons, 21
Emilio, Captain Luis Fenollosa, 102
Epstein, Diana, 26, 105, 117

Faberge, Carl, 114
Ferdinand, Francis (Archduke of Austria), 4
Flapper buttons, 49, 91, 186
Francis I (King of France), 140
Franklin, Benjamin, 114, 149, 183
Frederick II (King of Prussia), 84
Freedom buttons, 30, 90
Frost, Robert, 170, 173

Gaulle, Charles de, 117
George II (King of England), 143
George III (King of England), 67, 84, 114, 162, 189
Gilroy, John, 26
Goodyear, Charles, 127
Green, Marilyn, 79, 193
Gwinnett, Button, 146

Hancock, John, 23
Handel, George Frederick, 3
Handkerchief buttons, 36, 48, 87–88
Hat buttons (Chinese Mandarin), 152, 166
Henry III (King of England), 89, 129, 157, 158
Henry VIII (King of England), 36, 140, 141, 158
Henry IV (King of France), 159

Jackson, Andrew, 3, 22–23, 137

Kennedy, Jacqueline, 93
Koumphiphobia, 6–7, 194

Lafayette, Marquis Marie Joseph de, 92
Landers, Ann, 80, 156
Lewis, Meriwether, 57
Lincoln, Abraham, 23, 130, 152
Livery buttons, 28
Louis IX (King of France), 157, 189
Louis XIV (King of France), 88, 91, 143, 159, 192
Louis XV (King of France), 14
Louis XVI (King of France), 45, 56, 141–142, 143
Ludwig II (King of Bavaria), 143–144

Mary, Queen of Scots, 36, 141, 189
Medici Family, 13
Memorial buttons, 28, 89–90, 122
Montgolfier brothers, 5
Mourning buttons, 28, 89, 112, 136
Mozart, Wolfgang Amadeus, 114
Murphy buttons, 33

Napoleon I (Emperor of France), 4, 28, 37, 54, 84, 114
Napoleon III (Emperor of France), 88, 146
Netsukes, 47
Noriega, Felicidad, 6

Old Button Shop, 60
Osborne, Peggy Ann, 109

Paar, Jack, 116
Pants buttons, 21
Patterson, Gertrude, 102
Pearly Kings and Queens, 37–38, 77, 109–110, 145
Peep-hole buttons, 17
Perfume buttons, 16, 18, 126
Peter I (Czar of Russia), 113
Philip (Duke of Edinburgh), 33
Pin-back buttons, 154–156
Poison buttons, 13, 19
Political buttons, 17, 21–23, 129
Potter, Beatrix, 9, 171
Presley, Elvis, 10

Pushkin, Alexander, 4

Reagan, Ronald, 92
Rebus buttons, 45, 129
Reflector buttons, 20–21
Renaissance Buttons (shop), 52
Revere, Paul, 113
Revolution, American, 14, 133
Rie, Dame Lucie, 114
Rivers, Joan, 120

Safro, Millicent, 50, 79, 105, 117, 122
San Jacinto, Battle of, 9
Schiaparelli, Elsa, 113, 145
Scott, Sir Walter, 52, 170
Shakespeare, William, 128, 165–166
Shields, Brooke, 117
Silver John the Bonesetter, 6–7
Sluts (candle buttons), 46
Smuggler's buttons, 14
Speights, M. W. "Freddie," 10, 107
Stanhope buttons, 18
Stein, Gertrude, 175
Stevens, Dalton, 78, 106, 145
Stewart, Martha, 151
Streisand, Barbra, 119
Studs (lapel buttons), 85, 153
Syd, the parrot, 34

Taylor, Zachary, 68
Temple, Shirley, 120
Tender Buttons (shop), 5, 24, 26, 52, 79, 105, 116, 149
Tingue, Senator John, 99–100, 110
Tintype buttons, 90
Truman, Bess, 74
Twain, Mark, 169, 174–175

Victoria (Queen of England), 85, 89, 100, 112

War of 1812, 132–133
Warther Museum, 106, 110
Washington, George, 92, 105, 113, 173, 188, 196
Weingarten, Lucille, 147, 150
Wilder, Laura Ingalls, 170
Williston Seminary, 10, 195
Wolfe, Tom, 117–118
World War I, 4, 15, 20, 131, 136–137, 179

About the Author

Ellaraine Lockie writes nonfiction books, magazine articles, columns, children's stories and award-winning poetry. She lives in Northern California with her husband and collections of animals and buttons.

About the Illustrator

Heather Lockie is a free-lance artist, teacher and musician whose work has appeared in books, magazines and on compact disc covers. She lives in Southern California with her cats when she isn't on tour with her band.